ROUTINES AND TRANSITIONS

Routines & Transitions

A Guide for Early Childhood Professionals

Nicole Malenfant

Translated by Selma Tischer and Richard Streiling

Redleaf Press
www.redleafpress.org

Published by Redleaf Press
a division of Resources for Child Caring
10 Yorkton Court
St. Paul, MN 55117
Visit us online at www.redleafpress.org.

First edition 2006
Cover design, interior design, and typesetting by Percolator
Cover photos by Steve Wewerka
Interior photos by Nicole Malenfant and Steve Wewerka
The interior of this book was typeset in Adobe Garamond Pro, Electra, and Scala Sans.
Printed in the United States of America

13 12 11 10 09 08 07 06   1 2 3 4 5 6 7 8

Redleaf Press books are available at a special discount when purchased in bulk for special premiums and sales promotions. For details, contact the sales manager at 800-423-8309.

Library of Congress Cataloging-in-Publication Data

Malenfant, Nicole.
    [Routines et transitions en services éducatifs. English]
    Routines and transitions : a guide for early childhood professionals / Nicole Malenfant ; translated by Selma Tischer and Richard Streiling.—1st ed.
        p. cm.
    Includes bibliographical references.
    ISBN-13: 978-1-933653-04-4
    ISBN-10: 1-933653-04-3
    1. Early childhood education—Activity programs. 2. Education, Preschool—Activity programs. 3. Child development. I. Title.
LB1139.35.A37M35713 2006
372.21—dc22

                                        2006014277

Printed on acid-free paper.

Routines & Transitions

Acknowledgments xi
Introduction 1

▨ **Chapter 1: Theoretical Framework** **3**

1.1 Childhood: A crucial period of life 4
1.2 The importance of early childhood education 5
1.3 Frame of reference: Democratic pedagogy 5
1.4 Routine and transition activities in early childhood education programs 6
    A. What is a routine activity? 7
    B. What is a transition activity? 8
1.5 Summary of the democratic approach applied to routine and transition activities 8
    A. Human environment strategies 8
    B. Physical environment strategies 9
    C. Time management strategies 9
    D. Strategies to meet children's true needs 10
    E. Strategies that promote educational values 10

▨ **Chapter 2: General Strategies** **11**

2.1 Planning and organization 12
2.2 Preventing problematic situations 13
2.3 Scheduling daily activities 13
2.4 Ensuring children's safety 15
2.5 Managing time 15
2.6 Balancing new and familiar activities 16
2.7 Organizing the physical space 16
2.8 Controlling noise 17
2.9 Minimizing waiting time 18
2.10 Minimizing large group gatherings and movements 18
2.11 Encouraging children to participate 19
2.12 Offering choices 19
2.13 Ensuring consistency 20
2.14 Building a game bank 20
2.15 Planning the end of activities 20
2.16 Considering children in context 20
2.17 Analyzing successes and difficulties 21
2.18 Giving clear verbal directions 22
2.19 Modulating your voice 23

2.20 Taking direct action 23
2.21 Staying close to the children 23
2.22 Using make-believe 23
2.23 Avoiding the expectation of perfection at all costs 24
2.24 Getting the children's attention 24
2.25 Using positive reinforcement 24
2.26 Refocusing the children 25
2.27 Encouraging individual thinking 25
2.28 Showing perseverance and optimism 26
2.29 Showing flexibility 26
2.30 Ensuring the well-being of educators 26

Chapter 3: Hygiene 27

3.1 Hand washing 28
    A. Materials and equipment 28
    B. When to wash hands 28
    C. Hand-washing technique 30
    D. Setting a good example 30
    E. Hand-washing training 30
    F. Games 31
    G. Songs 32
3.2 Toothbrushing 32
    A. When to brush teeth 32
    B. Materials and equipment 33
    C. Toothbrushing techniques 33
    D. Games and tricks 34
3.3 Bathroom routine 34
    A. Bathroom use 34
    B. Diaper changing 35
    C. Hygiene and sanitation 36
    D. Saying the right thing at the right time 36
3.4 Nose blowing 36
    A. When to blow noses 36
    B. Materials and equipment 37
    C. Nose-blowing techniques 37

Chapter 4: Snacks and Meals 39

4.1 Healthy diet 40
4.2 Children's typical food preferences 40
4.3 Managing the task of meals and snacks 41
4.4 Physical and material organization 44
4.5 Creating a positive mealtime atmosphere 45
4.6 Mealtimes with two-year-olds 46
4.7 Lack of appetite, refusal to eat, and other challenges 47
    A. Eating patterns and children's temperaments 47
    B. Eating patterns at different ages 48
    C. Observing children's eating patterns 48
    D. Individual eating habits 49

E. Useful meal and snack strategies 49
F. Emotions and eating habits 51
G. Food preferences 51
H. Fluctuating appetites 51
4.8 Eating habits and special diets 51
4.9 Overeating 51
4.10 Table manners 52
4.11 Allergies and food intolerance 53
4.12 Choking dangers 54
4.13 Nutrition education 55
A. Encouraging children's participation during meals 55
B. Food awareness 55
C. Introducing nutrition throughout the curriculum 56
1.) Food theme at circle time 56
2.) Food-themed activities 56
3.) Materials for dramatic play 57
4.) Educational field trips 57
5.) Other games 57

Chapter 5: Nap or Relaxation Time — **59**

5.1 The need to rest and refresh the body and the mind 60
5.2 Children's sleep patterns 60
A. Naptime for children who sleep 61
B. Naptime for children who do not sleep 61
5.3 Requests from parents 62
5.4 Room arrangement 65
5.5 Materials and equipment 65
5.6 Preparation and implementation 66
5.7 Getting up from nap 68
5.8 Other factors that affect nap and rest time 68
5.9 Games to introduce rest time 69

Chapter 6: Dressing and Undressing — **71**

6.1 Equipment and organization 72
6.2 Duration 73
6.3 Upon arrival and departure and when going outside and coming back in 73
6.4 Factors that make dressing and undressing easier 73
A. Adapted clothing 74
B. Adapted tasks 74
6.5 Little games 74

Chapter 7: Tidying and Cleaning Up — **77**

7.1 A practical storage system 78
A. The area and the equipment 78
B. Getting children to help 80
C. Tidying the outdoor space 80
D. Labeling 81

7.2 Cleaning up 81
7.3 How you can encourage tidy-up and cleanup 82
    A. Planning the display of games and materials 82
    B. Having realistic expectations 82
    C. Fostering learning 84
    D. Giving advance warning 84
    E. Managing time 85
    F. Providing positive reinforcement 85
    G. Letting children bear the consequences 85
    H. Being active 85
    I. Encouraging ongoing tidy-up 86
7.4 Tidy-up and clean-up games 86
    A. A job for everyone 86
    B. Three cheers for creativity! 86
    C. A bit of complicity 86
    D. Dusting 86
    E. Counting 86
    F. Magical vacuum cleaner 87
    G. What do you want to put away? 87
    H. Music time! 87
    I. Parallel play for the end of cleanup 87
    J. A challenge for you 87
    K. Timing 87
    L. Relay cleanup 87
    M. One demonstration equals a thousand explanations 87
    N. Speaking toys 87
    O. Ways to move around 87
    P. "Simon says" 87
7.5 Clean-up songs 87

▉ Chapter 8: Group and Circle Time   89

8.1 Grouping children 90
8.2 Encouraging children to participate 90
8.3 Encouraging children to get into a group 90
8.4 Where to group children 91

▉ Chapter 9: Group Movements   93

9.1 Strategies to avoid waiting times 94
9.2 Reducing large group movements 94
9.3 Ensuring children's safety 94
9.4 Little games 95

▉ Chapter 10: Arrival and Departure   97

10.1 A warm and personal welcome 98
10.2 Saying hello with a smile 99
10.3 Calling children by their first names 100
10.4 Staff stability 100

10.5 Helping children and parents separate at the beginning of the day 100
10.6 Taking attendance 101
10.7 Helping children and parents leave 101
10.8 Dealing with parents who are late for pickup 102
10.9 Little games 102

▌ Chapter 11: Unavoidable Waiting **103**

11.1 Countering unavoidable waits 104
11.2 Organizing unavoidable waits 105
11.3 Making the best of the situation 106
    A. Verbal games 106
    B. Visual observation games 108
    C. Listening games 108
    D. Hand-eye coordination games 109
    E. Symbolic games/role play 109
    F. Audiovisual games 110
    G. Fine-motor games 110
    H. Gross-motor games 110
    I. Breathing games 111
    J. Olfactory games 111
    K. Tactile games 111
    L. Vocal games 112
    M. Artistic games 112
    N. Self-massage 113

References 115

Acknowledgments

Writing a book about early childhood education has been a dream of mine for a long time. If today this dream has become reality, it is in great part due to the determination my parents passed on to me, and I am greatly indebted to them. My gratitude goes next to the students I was privileged to meet as a teacher and field supervisor at the Collège Édouard-Montpetit. Several of these students were a rich source of ideas and thoughts that inspired the writing of this manual.

Heartfelt thanks to the representatives of the future of humanity, the children of early childhood education programs, who welcomed me with open arms. I cherish their spontaneity and their refreshing authenticity.

Many thanks for all the passionate specialists in the early childhood education field who listened patiently to me when I was undertaking this project: my colleagues, as well as Diane Poudrier, an early childhood education teacher at Vanier College, who helped me with her judicious comments in the process of preparing an English edition.

I would like to thank Dominique Léger, who created the beautiful illustrations.

I am very grateful to Selma Tischer, who, with the help of Richard Streiling, translated the work into English. Her encouragement and professionalism greatly facilitated my work.

I am also grateful to Ville-Marie and Enfranfreluche child care center educators, who very kindly suggested songs.

Let me also mention the following people who welcomed me into their child care centers and allowed me to take pictures: Lise Fréchette and her team, Les Faucons de St. Mathieu; Louise Bourque, head of home day care services Mamie-Pom; and the teams of the child care centers at Porculus, Pierre-Boucher, La Ruche, Mon Petit-Édouard, Pour vos Tout-p'tits de Longueuil, Au pied du Mont, L'Apprenti-Sage, and Pomme Soleil.

Finally, I am indebted to Sid Farrar, editor-in-chief at Redleaf Press, for his sustained and sincere interest in this project.

Introduction

I've had many opportunities to observe early childhood education programs since I started working with children in these programs in the early 1980s. My passion for children and for the field of education were kindled in those early years, and have continued to grow through teaching children of various ages and teaching adult educators, as well as through reading and coursework. This book is the result of numerous contacts with early childhood programs through my work as an educator, college professor, consultant, and fieldwork supervisor. Its content is based on practical experience within a theoretical framework.

My experience has convinced me of the educational value of basic skills necessary for routine and transition activities. I have often witnessed educators in action with their groups of children. Without question, educators can greatly influence children's development through pedagogical activities repeated day after day, hour after hour. Consider how educators help children to progressively become independent through basic life skills such as dressing, eating, and hygiene routines. Educators also help children learn the rules of group living and develop language and social skills. Learning such skills is not a matter of chance. It is in fact highly dependent on the professional competency of educational staff. Harmonious learning of these basic life skills also requires close cooperation with parents.

Considering the incredible quantity of routine and transition activities performed in an early childhood program, we should give them an important place in the early childhood curriculum. This is why I hope that a reference book on routines and transitions will be a useful pedagogical tool for early childhood educators. It will also be of value for students in early childhood education, or for anyone undertaking in-service training in early childhood education, whether directly or indirectly, as an educator, manager, or parent.

My suggestions are certainly neither infallible nor magic recipes. Rather, they are meant to provide guidelines for a reflective practice.

The age span covered in this work is two to eight years old and is referred to as *early childhood*.

The book is composed of eleven chapters. The first two chapters explain the theoretical framework of democratic pedagogy as it relates to routines and transitions. They also give a general overview of the organization and implementation of routine and transition activities.

The next nine chapters cover the following routines: hand washing, toothbrushing, bathroom, nose blowing, snacks, meals, naptime or relaxation, and dressing and undressing. They also cover the following transition activities: tidying and cleaning up, group gatherings, arrival and departure, and unavoidable waiting.

The term *educator* refers to anyone assuming an educational role with children. Today's reality is that the personnel taking care of young children in early childhood settings are mainly women. Therefore, the feminine form has been used throughout to represent educators of both genders, with the sole purpose of making the text easier to read. To equitably represent children of both genders, I have alternated between masculine and feminine pronouns.

The terms *early childhood program* and *child care center* have been chosen to designate the different types of early childhood settings. They include child care centers, family (or home) child care, drop-in centers, and preschools. The information in this book can also be useful for managing routines and transitions in kindergarten and other educational programs for children up to eight years old.

I use the term *parent* to refer to anyone having the primary responsibility for a child: father, mother, grandparent, guardian, and so forth.

1

Theoretical Framework

CHAPTER CONTENTS

1.1 Childhood: A crucial period of life

1.2 The importance of early childhood education

1.3 Frame of reference: Democratic pedagogy

1.4 Routine and transition activities in early childhood education programs

    A. What is a routine activity?

    B. What is a transition activity?

1.5 Summary of the democratic approach applied to routine and transition activities

    A. Human environment strategies

    B. Physical environment strategies

    C. Time management strategies

    D. Strategies to meet children's true needs

    E. Strategies that promote educational values

Most people agree that the first years of life are significant determinants in a person's development. Also, it's known that the fulfillment of a child's potential is not the fruit of chance. In the domains of physical, psychomotor, intellectual, social, and affective development, children are subjected to numerous influences that can, in large part, be controlled. Several studies emphasize the positive influence of quality early childhood programs, whether those programs are home or family child care settings, child care centers, preschools, or other types of programs. We also know that many children spend a large part of their childhood in such programs, sometimes more than two thousand hours a year. It is essential, therefore, to provide excellent services that offer quality activities. Among these activities, routine and transition activities take up more than half of the schedule.

1.1 Childhood: A crucial period of life

It would be inconceivable to write a book on routine and transition activities in early childhood programs without first broaching the topic of childhood. This book does so in simple terms, without focusing on the main early childhood development theories discussed at length in many texts.

Through the centuries, following the evolution of societies, the concepts of *children* and *childhood* have changed often. Children have sometimes been seen as incomplete beings without intelligence or as cheap labor, and at other times they have been thought of as kings and queens, mysterious beings, or the promise of a better future. Regardless of historical period, children have always been treated differently from adults (Papalia, Olds, and Feldman 1998).

Only recently has scientific inquiry shed light on the nature of childhood and its obvious repercussions on the whole life of the individual. As of the beginning of the twenty-first century, childhood is considered to be a time not only to grow physically but also to learn and to prepare for the future. The creation of youth protection laws, the UNESCO adoption of the Convention on the Rights of the Child (November 20, 1989), the establishment of community services supporting families, and the development of educational child care programs and play materials adapted to children bear witness to the intrinsic value of childhood. Even if the cause of children's rights remains an unfinished mission, its goal can be pursued, anchored in a solid foundation of research and values.

It is ideal for children to live their childhoods in confidence, surrounded by responsible, conscientious, and benevolent adults. Subconsciously, every child longs to be considered a person worthy of respect, with his own story and personality. Our knowledge of children's needs and an increased awareness of the importance of early childhood education are considerable influences on the educational methods that contribute to children's development. Early childhood educators will continually learn about children through professional resources, exchanges, and training, as well as through their regular and systematic observations of children.

All children have a need for security, hugs, stimulation, encouragement, and guidance. No matter what their origin, children should have the right to laugh, cry, feel vulnerable, get attached, move, explore, be frustrated, affirm themselves, sing, show pride, love life, and count on adults to defend their needs in order to grow in peace. Children are neither small adults nor defenseless beings. They are human beings in their own right, with incredible potential that we need to nurture as much as possible.

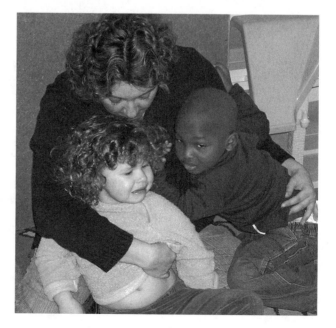

The definition of *childhood* is not limited by development standards or statistics. It is first and foremost a dynamic and continuous process that encompasses an inevitable transformation of the person. It is the job of adults to foster this process in the most positive way possible (Legendre 1993, 453).

1.2 The importance of early childhood education

With the social and family changes that have occurred in recent years, early childhood education is not limited to the family but encompasses society as represented by child care centers, preschools, and family or home child care. Early childhood education is fast becoming a specialty distinct from the psychology and education domains. More and more it is discussed in newspapers, radio and television reports, public debates, and conferences and on the Internet. Despite this evolution, the term *education* is too often limited to school learning, as if early childhood education in a child care center were a less serious business. Too many people still believe that education outside of a formal school setting consists of keeping children busy until they are old enough to enter school. Although erroneous, this concept of early childhood education remains deeply anchored in people's minds. Hence, it is important to spread knowledge about activities in early childhood settings, because doing so directly affects the well-being of children and influences early learning, which, in turn, forms the basis of later school success.

> *If parents are experts on their children, then the educator is the specialist of early childhood development within the context of group life.*

Even before children enter the "big school" they are capable of reproducing the essential behaviors of daily life that determine, in large part, the autonomy of a person. They learn to walk, talk, eat, and drink alone, get dressed and undressed, go to the bathroom, and perform appropriate hygiene care such as washing hands and brushing teeth. Children also learn to manage some social situations, such as expressing their needs, making choices, solving problems at their own level, and respecting the rules of group life. These skills are, in many cases, learned through the numerous activities offered in early childhood educational programs. Through such active experiences, children have the opportunity to develop in a comprehensive way as they prepare for the next stage of life.

1.3 Frame of reference: Democratic pedagogy

With the advent of psychological research and the development of more humane practices during the twentieth century, education theorists and practitioners have come to oppose the traditional, encyclopedic pedagogy that emphasizes knowledge, technical learning, and direct preparation for school learning. Rather, they promote a child-centered pedagogy focused on the whole development of children. Even though this approach was conceived by Jean-Jacques Rousseau in the eighteenth century, it was some 150 years before the development in Europe of the "New School" movement associated with Freinet, Montessori, and Decroly. In North America, the effects of this more open pedagogy started to be felt only in the 1960s, becoming more prominent in the 1970s.

Child psychology is a relatively new science. Piaget, with his cognitive development theory, has had the most influence on childhood education. Bettelheim, Freud, Erikson, and Vygotsky, as well as pediatricians such as Dolto, Brazelton, Dodson, and Gordon, all influenced, in one way or another, the concepts of child-centered education and active learning, upon which many educational programs today are based. Other proven programs include the Developmentally Appropriate Practice (DAP) program from the National Association for the Education of Young Children (NAEYC), the Bank Street Model (Developmental Interaction Approach), and the High/Scope program. Several components of the New School are inherent to the *Jouer c'est magique* (Play is magical) program created for child care services by the Quebec government.

The framework proposed here focuses on the true needs of children while fostering their whole development. Because children learn better when their basic needs are met, we make more room for eating, resting, and hygiene times. In this holistic view, children actively participate in their own evolution and in their own life. This contrasts with both the autocratic approach, in which children are forced to meet the expectations of authority figures, and, at the other end of the spectrum, the free pedagogy approach, which leaves children alone to face choices they are not always able to make and to carry through.

> *The pedagogical approach of this text uses routine and transition activities to prepare children for life, to stimulate them to learn, and to guide them in developing their capacities and their talents, while respecting their unique styles and their own rhythms. We call this democratic pedagogy.*

Faced with the multiple names used to describe a pedagogy centered on children realizing their potential, this text uses the term *democratic approach*. The reason for favoring this model for planning and organizing routine and transition activities is that it is an excellent method to respond to the needs of today's children—children who will have to build the world of tomorrow. See Box 1.1.

BOX 1.1 Characteristics of the democratic approach

- Primacy is given to the whole development of the child.
- Adults respect the physical, psychological, social, and cultural particularities of children, and their true needs.
- The value of play in the process of learning is inestimable.
- Children's active participation in both the big and the small daily tasks is important.
- Partnership with families is a necessity.

In the context of the *democratic approach*, learning is a synergistic process in which one aspect of development—physical and psychomotor, social and affective, or cognitive—stimulates another.

For example, a child might get interested in a new food, such as mangos, by observing an educator eating some and listening to a story about the fruit. In this way, language, imagination, understanding, sensory perceptions, affective relationships, and nutritional needs act in synergy to present a new experience for the child.

Play is the natural way children understand the world around them. Routine and transition activities give them many occasions to learn while playing: to play at putting on clothes in the right order with the help of an action song; to play at returning the toys to their "home"; to play at moving without making noise, like a little mouse. It is through play that children learn basic abilities.

Each child is a distinct human being worthy of a thorough and detailed study, without categorizing her according to age, origin, or gender. When we consider a child as a unique being, we respect her individuality and culture while encouraging her to adapt to group life. We encourage her to make choices and foster her self-esteem. We help her to express her needs and we help her try to meet them according to her capabilities. This approach requires a knowledge of child development as well as systematic observation of the child, because children and the world around them are constantly changing.

Despite the importance given to children in the context of democratic pedagogy, parents and early childhood educators also assume a crucial role in promoting children's potential, acting as guides, supports, and mediators. Parental cooperation is essential to the success of this pedagogical approach. Educational settings must develop a means to foster partnerships with families. In relation to routine and transition activities in educational settings, the democratic approach is a set of conscious dynamic actions inspired by the constant probing and reflection of educators. Through appropriate educational choices, educators allow children to learn according to their developmental stage, rhythm, and reality.

1.4 Routine and transition activities in early childhood education programs

Life in an early childhood program is packed with activities that promote the development of the whole child. Several of these activities are repeated day after day and provide a frame of reference for the day's organization. These are *routine and transition activities*. Despite the large amount of time that is spent daily on these activities, they are not always valued at the same level as teacher-initiated curriculum activities, group time, and even free play. Regardless, the educator has to organize and lead several basic life tasks such as snacks, hand and mouth hygiene, nap preparation, and dressing.

Despite being repetitious, routine and transition activities are not trivial. On the contrary, there is much to do and learn during these moments. Early childhood programs offer children many opportunities to develop a wide range of skills necessary to their development: autonomy, verbal expression, self-knowledge, self-esteem, group living, and so forth. In many ways, routine and transition activities are as essential and important as more-recognized educational activities such as language stimulation, logic games, art, hand-eye coordination, and gross-motor games and activities.

Well-informed early childhood educators know how to use routines and transitions to promote the well-being of children in their care and how to teach those children awareness of their own basic needs: eating to care for one's body, resting to reenergize, wearing a hat for sun protection, and so forth. While maintaining physical and emotional safety and even the health of children, these educators maximize the value of routine and transition activities by generating a warm, comfortable atmosphere in which children master basic life skills at their own pace. Such educators are skilled professionals. They are not simply babysitters minding children. Such basic care of children is not just a mechanical function requiring limited knowledge and abilities. It is the main purpose of the day, requiring specific knowledge and skills.

Infants and preschool children may spend up to 55 hours a week in an early childhood program, or 2,640 hours annually, for a total of more than 13,200 hours through the preschool years. During this time, children learn basic skills they will use throughout their lives—skills necessary to half of the daily life of adults (eating, sleeping, walking, getting dressed, communicating, and so forth). "The key is to think through each part of the routine from a developmental perspective" (Brickman and Taylor 1991, 43).

On top of the official "program" of activities (sensory activities, motor activities, thematic activities, language stimulation, educational outings, free play, outdoor play), basic activities and routines benefit children's development. Likely more than 50 percent of the time in early childhood educational settings is dedicated to routine and transition activities (80 percent with children 0–2 years), about 1,320 hours or more per year. This means that during their preschool years (0–5 years), a child in a child care setting spends 6,600 hours performing routine and transition activities outside of the home. These numbers speak for themselves: they reveal the important role played by these moments in the life of a child and the necessity to devote attention to these routines and transitions.

For the educator, routine and transition activities constitute a special opportunity for personal contact with each and every child. Upon children's arrival or departure or during nap or snack time, an educator devotes attention to the children as she communicates with them through words and smiles. (However, at these times, children may oppose the adult because of fatigue or difficulty in changing activities.) Transitions also provide the opportunity to practice language skills and encourage children to communicate with their peers. There is a lot of time for chatting during snacks, dressing, or undressing. These activities also provide opportunities to solve conflicts or to develop greater physical autonomy.

A. WHAT IS A ROUTINE ACTIVITY?

A *routine activity* within an educational setting is a predictable basic activity that has to be performed daily. Such activities are generally scheduled at a fixed time and form the core of the day. A large number of routine activities are aimed at meeting basic needs such as eating, drinking, eliminating, resting, breathing calmly, maintaining good hygiene, keeping warm, and so forth. The younger the child, the longer these routine tasks take, and the more frequently they occur. These tasks also require greater attention from an adult. The best-known routine activities with young children include:

- Hygiene: hand washing, toothbrushing, toilet routines, and nose wiping
- Snacks and meals

- Nap or relaxation time
- Dressing and undressing

Beyond meeting physiological needs, routine activities contribute to the emotional well-being of children. They help children acquire time awareness by making them anticipate what will come next. They foster a feeling of security essential to trust building.

B. WHAT IS A TRANSITION ACTIVITY?

Transition activities are usually simple and brief. They are meant to connect two longer activities. They serve to regulate and punctuate the day. These moments announce a change, either of activities, of area, of play partners, or of educators. They include:

- Tidying and cleaning up
- Gathering in a group
- Group movement
- Arrivals and departures
- Unavoidable waiting periods

A good transition makes a connection between activities. Transitions respect the rhythm of children as much as possible and encourage children's participation and autonomy according to their stage of development. They are easy to set up and require little or no materials.

Transitions require particular attention from educators to organize the sequence of activities in a harmonious way. Careful planning of the sequence of activities and creative use of the time between activities limit the tensions and upheavals within a group of children.

1.5 Summary of the democratic approach applied to routine and transition activities

Learning specific behaviors such as eating neatly, buttoning up a coat, putting toys away, moving around calmly, or waiting patiently in the entryway depends upon the quality of the interventions made by the educator. Safety, access to educators, reassuring guidance, self-control, and adequate organization are essential for children to get through routines and transitions in the most positive way possible. These times often try the patience and the creativity of early childhood educators. Just think of getting children dressed in winter in cold climates, when children have to be coaxed into putting on snowsuits, mittens, boots, and hats, all in a limited time to avoid traffic jams in the entryway and children getting impatient. How many times do educators repeat the same instructions? "Hurry up—the others are ready to go out." "Hurry up—I already asked you three times to get dressed." How many stressful events can take place when helping two-year-olds get dressed? One cries and asks the educator to take her into her arms, another has a runny nose, and two dash out of the entryway. These transitions are demanding and stressful for both educators and children.

The following set of educational strategies—human environment, physical environment, time management, children's needs, and educational values—helps to ensure harmonious routine and transition activities while respecting the needs of each child. (See Figure 1.1 at the end of this chapter.)

A. HUMAN ENVIRONMENT STRATEGIES

- Ensure the stability of the educators.
- Foster continuity between home and the child care setting to minimize adaptation difficulties. Initiate a partnership between the family and the educational staff to foster continuity between both environments.
- Create situations where children can act on their own as much as possible. For instance, teach children how to wash their hands effectively at the sink instead of wiping the

- Give clear directions and follow them up with consistency and judgment.
- Encourage children's autonomy according to their abilities and the context. For instance, some children may benefit from self-service at meals, while others need help.
- Turn routines and transitions into games to get the children attentive and interested.
- Foster the progressive learning of social competencies tailored to the children's ages and abilities: interactions with peers, integration with other age groups, sharing, and so forth.
- Help children three and older develop self-discipline by encouraging them to manage their conflicts and understand the consequences of unacceptable behaviors while at the same time teaching them to recognize the validity of their acceptable behaviors. Make them aware of the consequences of their actions for themselves and for others.
- Encourage children to find solutions to problems. For example, help four-year-old Justin, who has difficulty accepting children other than his friends, find a compromise that will satisfy himself and a fellow student.
- Consider the direct or indirect suggestions made by children. For example, celebrate the end of tidy-up time in a way suggested by one of the children.

B. PHYSICAL ENVIRONMENT STRATEGIES

- Control the level of noise: use calm voices, install sound-absorbing materials, and limit the number of children at one place.
- Organize space so that it is safe, attractive, well lighted, well ventilated, and well kept.
- Limit the number of children per room.
- Set up a relaxation corner that children can easily access. Plan several key periods during the day when children can choose play materials that are conducive to relaxation.
- Organize the room so that it encourages initiative and a feeling of belonging. Display children's drawings and pictures on the walls.
- Plan various areas in cooperation with the children, according to their level of development.
- Take into account children's reaction when introducing unavoidable changes.
- Keep children safe at all times: respect the rules concerning the number of children allowed, make emergency numbers and first-aid kits easily accessible, and be aware of the evacuation procedure.
- Ensure that all materials are safe, tidily stored, stimulating and varied, adapted to the developmental level of the children, and available according to their needs.
- Get safe and comfortable furniture adapted to the size of the users, whether children or adults.

C. TIME MANAGEMENT STRATEGIES

- Plan an activity schedule that is both structured and flexible and that allows for enough time to complete routine and transition activities in a relaxed way.
- Reduce time constraints as much as possible.
- Alternate between physical and nonphysical activities, and between activities that require concentration and relaxing ones.
- Balance large group, small group, and individual activities.
- Plan child-initiated activities as well as teacher-initiated ones according to the children's needs.
- Ensure a balance between indoor and outdoor activities.

D. STRATEGIES TO MEET CHILDREN'S TRUE NEEDS

- Ensure that the basic needs of the children are met: they need to eat, drink, eliminate, rest, breathe healthy air, and spend time in natural light. In fulfilling these physical needs, respect their basic rhythms. Ensure that the children spend their time in a spacious environment where they can have fun, play, move, and have healthy outlets for their emotions.

- Give children the opportunity to learn how to take care of themselves and how to be comfortable. What are the signs of fatigue and discomfort?

- Encourage children to increase their self-esteem. Value their personal successes and strengths. Avoid comparisons and obsessions with performance and finished products.

- Refer on a regular basis to theoretical knowl-edge that sheds light on children's behavior.

- Facilitate social adaptation: closeness with adults, friendships with peers, development of sexual identity, and continuity of signifi-cant adults who are good models.

- Foster curiosity, creativity, and a sense of won-der in children, even in the simplest tasks.

E. STRATEGIES THAT PROMOTE EDUCATIONAL VALUES

- Enforce the values of the democratic approach: the well-being, self-esteem, autonomy, and uniqueness of each child.

- Regularly assess educational actions to ensure that they are consistent with these values.

The next chapter addresses these strategies in detail to better illustrate the basis of the demo-cratic approach in the context of routine and tran-sition activities.

FIGURE 1.1 **Democratic approach applied to routine and transition activities**

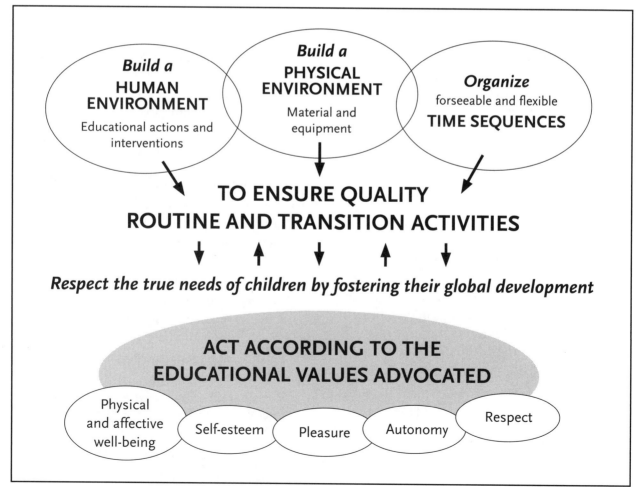

2

General Strategies

C H A P T E R   C O N T E N T S

2.1 Planning and organization

2.2 Preventing problematic situations

2.3 Scheduling daily activities

2.4 Ensuring children's safety

2.5 Managing time

2.6 Balancing new and familiar activities

2.7 Organizing the physical space

2.8 Controlling noise

2.9 Minimizing waiting time

2.10 Minimizing large group gatherings and movements

2.11 Encouraging children to participate

2.12 Offering choices

2.13 Ensuring consistency

2.14 Building a game bank

2.15 Planning the end of activities

2.16 Considering children in context

2.17 Analyzing successes and difficulties

2.18 Giving clear verbal directions

2.19 Modulating your voice

2.20 Taking direct action

2.21 Staying close to the children

2.22 Using make-believe

2.23 Avoiding the expectation of perfection at all costs

2.24 Getting the children's attention

2.25 Using positive reinforcement

2.26 Refocusing the children

2.27 Encouraging individual thinking

2.28 Showing perseverance and optimism

2.29 Showing flexibility

2.30 Ensuring the well-being of educators

Improvising routines and transitions does not result in quality activities. Rather, quality routines and transitions are planned with experience and forethought. A primary role of educators is to ensure a smooth implementation of the numerous routine and transition activities that punctuate daily life in an early childhood education program. To be successful, educators need to ground the strategies described below in the theoretical foundation presented in chapter 1.

2.1 Planning and organization

Routine and transition activities must be planned in the same way as all other educational activities. To be beneficial and pleasant for all, they must be based upon the same educational principles.

Well-planned transitions make the difference between a difficult and a harmonious day for early childhood educators as well as for children (Hohmann and Weikart 1995). Well-planned transitions encourage learning, motivation, and interpersonal relationships in children, who are proud to acquire new abilities. A planning tool can be used to solve problematic situations. Even in the absence of problematic situations, a planning tool has numerous advantages for routines and transitions. Among others, it helps to gather observations of the group and of each child. This tool must be experimented with over a long enough period to enable the educator to zero in on its advantages and its limitations, and to allow for necessary modifications. Moreover, as situations change, it is necessary to update and refine the planning tool. See Figure 2.1 for an example.

FIGURE 2.1 **Example of planning and assessment model for transition activities**

STRATEGIES/ PERSON RESPONSIBLE	Tidying Up		Group Movements		Group Activities and Circle Time	
	Application	Assessment	Application	Assessment	Application	Assessment
Verbal cues (instructions) Who:						
Use of puppet Who:						
Gradual start to prevent waiting times Who:						
Song or rhyme Who:						
Use of imagination Who:						
Visual clues (pictures) Who:						

Indeed, it takes time and energy to plan routines and transitions. Planning will, however, minimize the time spent on disciplinary actions by anticipating difficult situations and by preparing strategies to increase the children's cooperation. Considering the time that routine and transition activities take up in a day, it is imperative to plan them at least as carefully as any other part of the day.

Keep in mind that planning has to allow for the unexpected. Indeed, educators must balance planning with spontaneity when taking into account the needs of children in an educational context.

2.2 Preventing problematic situations

There are many explanations for problems arising from routine and transition activities that need to be closely analyzed. One of the main sources of tension is many children in an enclosed physical space. To prevent problems, this must be dealt with. "The larger the group, the less learning, even

with the legal number of educators present" (Hendrick 1988, 37).

First, a systematic observation involving looking, decoding, and analyzing greatly helps to identify factors that contribute to the problem and to potential solutions. Second, minimizing staff turnover, establishing stable children's groups, and controlling noise levels are sure to improve the climate of routine and transition activities.

2.3 Scheduling daily activities

Stability and consistency are the cornerstones of routine and transition activities. When the course of the activities of the day is predictable, it enhances children's time awareness. A stable and regular schedule has two positive outcomes: first, it ensures that all planned activities are implemented, and second, it provides a frame of reference that increases the children's feelings of security. This is especially so for the younger ones. For some children, the greatest stability in their volatile lives is the predictability of their daily routines away from home (Tyminski 2006).

Around three years of age, children begin to internalize a schedule, to the end that they can differentiate routine and transition activities from the other activities of the day. Children will be motivated to get dressed faster to play outside when they are aware of the sequence of events. Anticipating what is coming makes children feel they are in control of what is happening. Without being rigid, a typical schedule provides a framework for daily activities. It also allows parents/caretakers to learn about what happens during the day. It's important to be aware of daily routines and to inform all staff about any change (Tyminski 2006).

Here is a sample schedule. Do not forget that it is given as an example only and that schedules should always be flexible.

Example of a child care center schedule
(Using the democratic pedagogy framework for a group of two- and three-year-old children.)

7:00 AM Gradual arrival of educators.
- Opening the center.
- Gradual arrival of children and their parents.
- Welcoming the children.

- Removing outerwear in the entryway.
- Multiage group gathering.
- Individual communication with parents/caretakers, including comments on the child's health.
- Announcement of a special activity (optional).
- Breakfast according to preset agreement between the center and the caretakers (optional).
- Quiet games requiring a minimum of supervision to allow educators to welcome other children and their parents/caretakers. Play material available to children.
- Tidying up with children's cooperation.

8:45 AM Moving and gathering the children in their own rooms with their assigned educators.

- Assigning the tasks of the day, such as the weather chart. (This should not be long or rigid. It should be based above all on the children's real interests.)

9:00 AM Hand washing, bathroom.

- Snack and group time conducted in a friendly and relaxed manner.

10:00 AM Applying sunscreen and getting dressed, if applicable.

- Outside or inside child-directed play, depending on the weather. Small group activities.

11:00 AM Tidying up, with children's cooperation.

- Going back inside and removing outdoor clothing, if applicable.
- Bathroom routine, hand washing.
- Getting ready for lunch.

11:30 AM Lunch in a friendly and relaxed atmosphere with the presence at the table of a regular educator.

12:15 PM Table and floor cleanup, with the children's cooperation.

- Toothbrushing.
- Bathroom routine.
- Face and hand washing.
- Setting up nap equipment and materials, with children's participation.
- Children's partial undressing by themselves (socks, shoes, and so forth).

- Quiet play at the same time, left to the choice of the children.
- Nap ritual: story, song, self-massage.

12:45 PM Naptime.

- Positive and relaxing atmosphere.
- Constant supervision by one or two educators, depending on the number of children.

1:45 PM Quiet play for children who are not sleeping.

- For educators: writing information and observations in each child's journal.

2:15 PM Waking up the children, while respecting their individual rhythms.

- Children getting dressed by themselves.
- Bathroom.
- Storing of bedding, with children's cooperation.
- Child-directed or free play, rotating the material once in a while.

3:00 PM Hand washing.

- Snack and group time.
- Applying sunscreen and getting dressed, if applicable.

3:45 PM Small group activities (inside or outside).

- Gradual gathering in the multi-age group.

4:30 PM Parents/caretakers start arriving.

- Children and educators start leaving.
- Personalized and warm welcome of parents/caretakers.

6:05 PM Closing of center.

- During the evening, home child care educators can plan the last details for the next day.
- Preparing snacks, materials, and so forth.
- Cleaning of bathrooms, potties, and so forth.

Television should be limited as much as possible in early childhood programs. Most children already spend about twenty hours a week in front of a screen at home.

There are many strategies to help children go through routines and transitions in a peaceful way. They include preparing materials needed for activities in advance, reducing waiting periods, and avoiding having many children at once doing the same activity. Children can be allowed to start activities at their own pace. For example, each child can start snack time individually as soon as she returns from the bathroom.

A chart that illustrates the sequence of daily activities with drawings or pictures can help children anticipate activities. A monthly wall calendar may be useful to show student visits, outings, and special events.

2.4 Ensuring children's safety

Safety first! That is our motto when working with children. Never take anything for granted, and supervise children at all times. Stay beyond reproach. Sadly, any accident occurring in a child care center is an accident that could have been avoided. A one-second lack of attention, a forgotten item, or an object that is poorly used may cause an injury. The frequency of injuries is linked directly to the quality of supervision (Pimento and Kernested 2004). It is true that children must be taught to be careful from their youngest days. However, educators have the prime responsibility for children's safety at all times. If rooms are shared with others, as is the case in home child care, safety takes extra effort. In the end, educators must always assume this responsibility for themselves rather than deferring it to others. To ensure

safety, consider space organization, selection and inspection of materials, activity planning, and noise reduction.

2.5 Managing time

Educators are responsible for time management so that children are not rushed, except in a few unavoidable situations.

Educators must take into account routine and transition activities to maximize the benefits of these privileged moments. A simple watch becomes an essential tool. By managing their time, educators will be more relaxed and more inclined to communicate with children, thereby gaining an awareness of individual needs. Sound time management eliminates unnecessary constraints such as rushing through snack time in a mere ten minutes. Indeed, it is preferable to start snack time a little before the official time to allow children to enjoy eating and communicating with their peers. Planning a realistic schedule for routine and transition activities will ensure success.

2.6 Balancing new and familiar activities

A careful balance between new and familiar activities is important, especially for toddlers who stubbornly cling to their routines. Try not to introduce too many changes too rapidly in their lives. Preschoolers are less disturbed by novelty. Avoid feelings of insecurity in children by introducing changes gradually. Older children can even participate in the change process by, for instance, taking on a simple responsibility or giving advice.

Changes can be introduced in stages once priorities have been identified. It is wise to solve only one problem at a time. Avoid implementing modifications on the spot.

2.7 Organizing the physical space

The physical organization of a room or of an outside play area tells a lot about the quality of the child care center. A physical setting that is warm, stimulating, comfortable, functional, and hospitable for parents and educators as well as for children will foster well-being, socialization, and individual responses to needs, as advocated by democratic pedagogy. All activities will benefit if bathrooms, activity centers, and coat hooks are conveniently located. Whenever possible, coat hooks need to be strategically located close to the exit to the outside play area. Room decorations—seasonal or child art—should not be overwhelming. Natural lighting should be plentiful but subdued whenever needed. Temperatures should be adjustable—not too warm, not too cold—and walls should feature neutral or subdued colors. Ideally, windows in all rooms should be open every day and in all seasons to ensure good ventilation.

"Staff should suspect the quality of the air in the building when people are frequently experiencing symptoms such as headaches, fatigue, dizziness, or irritation in eyes, nose or throat" (Pimento and Kernested 2004, 68).

It is no secret that environment has a big influence on children's behavior. A well-planned environment can minimize the need for disciplinary action. For example, a bench located in the bathroom provides the twenty or so children who must wait their turn a place to sit down, avoiding fatigue and scrambling.

In each room of a center, corners reserved for specific play must be clearly identified. These may include a psychomotor activity corner that harbors objects to push and pull, a relaxation corner with comfortable pillows and attractive books, and a storage corner for children's personal belongings. Each area should be identified by dividers or shelves of some kind. A color line on the floor may be used to define a specific space. Clear and functional divisions between areas—rest areas, play areas, circle areas, meal areas—foster harmony and calm.

> *Dividers must not prevent educators from being able to supervise all children adequately.*

Safety and a sense of security for children are of paramount importance. Dividers must be low, and, if possible, they should have see-through openings. They should be designed in such a way that they are not hazards.

A simple division between a house corner and a building corner may make a difference in play. In a large room, a clear division of the play area prevents the spillover of children and material. However, educators must always show flexibility by allowing children to carry material from one area to another to facilitate play. For instance, dress-up clothes can be carried from the play corner to the kitchen corner to act out a visit to a restaurant. Objects that can be used in more than one way should nevertheless be stored in a systematic way after use. Low furniture is also very useful and helps to foster autonomy: low shelves, with a maximum height of about 3 feet (1 meter); pockets and wallboards to store objects; and wheeled storage containers that allow children to take what they need. On the other hand, a vast and open space with materials out of children's reach is sure to foster boredom and dependence. Similarly, space cluttered with play material prevents movement and generates confusion and restlessness in children, and it may also lead to falls. Bear in mind that play spaces that might be disorderly during play time can be returned to order during subsequent tidy-up time. By returning all materials to their proper storage places, children will easily learn where to find them again.

A well-organized space presupposes giving children responsibilities. Children take pride in taking care of their environment. To achieve this, they must be able to easily find their way about. Helpful pictures and posters facilitate this. Everybody will get the message if clear rules and tips are posted. For instance, a detailed plan of where cots are to be placed for naptime could be posted on the closet where the cots are stored. Similarly, notes can be posted on all closed cupboards and closets to indicate what is stored there.

If children are to feel comfortable and "at home" in an environment, it is necessary to make available to them play material and equipment adapted to their needs and at their level of physical and motor, intellectual, communicative, socio-affective, and moral development.

> *The needs of children are at the center of any educational philosophy. Respecting children inevitably entails an attentive observation of their verbal and nonverbal reactions.*

The need to make a quiet corner, well isolated from noisy areas, available to children during at least part of the day cannot be overstressed. Such a space should be planned for outside as well as inside areas. It has to be separate from the area set up for naptime. A quiet corner allows children to relax and to get rid of the stress inherent in group life. The area may include a small upholstered sofa or armchair; a beanbag chair; cushions where children can sit, lie down, or play quietly without others interfering; a soft carpet; stuffed toys; and a see-through divider. Needless to say, it has to remain clean and safe.

> *Tidiness (without being extreme), safety, cleanliness, usefulness, protection against noise, and comfort are all characteristics of a well-managed environment in a child care setting.*

2.8 Controlling noise

The need to limit noise also cannot be overstressed. Noise generates concentration difficulties that may lead to real behavior and attention problems. The following materials may help absorb noise: porous materials, large pieces of cork fixed onto metal cabinets, carpets, tennis balls under the feet of chairs, decorative banners on the ceiling, and a small carpet in the construction/block play corner. The structure of the building probably cannot easily be modified, but whenever possible, select materials with the aim of reducing noise. Adults may try to restrict the movements of children to lower the decibels—they may ask children to push a chair slowly, to whisper, or to say sorry when they make too much noise. However, these are not valid solutions for noise problems. The most effective means to minimize noise is to reduce the number of children in a given space. One more word of caution: If background music plays for more than ten minutes, it tends to make speaking increasingly difficult and generally causes the noise level to rise.

The higher the noise level, the higher the restlessness of children, and the higher the number of guidance interventions. It is well known that noise raises stress levels, which in turn raises the level of noise. "A constant noise level can make people feel tired and irritable" (Pimento and Kernested 2004, 68). See Figure 2.2.

2.9 Minimizing waiting time

Children hate waiting, especially in silence. Moreover, many children do not learn to wait at home, because their caretakers usually respond rapidly to their needs. We all know that children who wait without doing anything get bored, agitated, and frustrated, and they often find a way to keep busy by using their peers for stimulation and distraction. Consequently, waiting has to be eliminated whenever possible. One of the ways to counter the negative effects of waiting is to keep children

busy with small tasks tailored to their abilities. If an educator is completing tasks while children are waiting, she increasingly will have to intervene to counteract boisterousness and impatience. Since children do not have the same time awareness as adults, five minutes of waiting time may appear endless.

Bathrooms and sinks located away from the room create waiting situations for children. Minimize waiting time for the bathroom by reducing large group movements. Five-year-olds are autonomous enough to go to the bathroom by themselves, even if the bathroom is located outside of the room. Another solution may be to take a small group to the bathroom while another educator supervises the children in the room. Even when going back inside after outside play, it is better to divide children into small groups.

2.10 Minimizing large group gatherings and movements

A general rule is to avoid situations where children must perform tasks all at the same time, since this generates boisterousness, stress, and noise. Lining up ten children who need to wash their hands at the same sink, for example, is sure to end in a noisy, restless, and aggressive group. Children, like adults, need at least a modicum of personal space to develop positive social skills.

FIGURE 2.2 **Influence of noise in an early chilhood program**

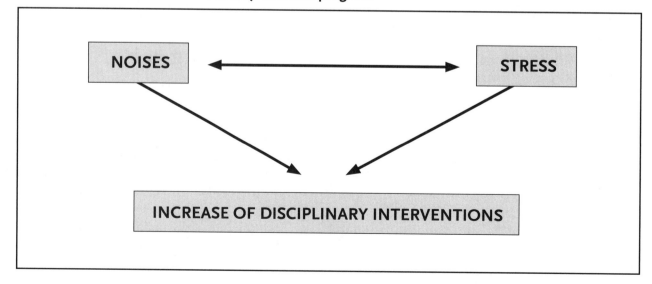

2.11 Encouraging children to participate

By sharing tasks with children every time a situation lends itself to do so, educators increase the individual attention they can give. Also, whenever children are allowed to share in tasks adapted to their abilities, they increase their sense of competency and their self-esteem, qualities that are essential to overall development. Such tasks include sweeping after lunch, helping educators put away lunch items, and so forth (Hendrick 1988). Self-esteem is built not by educators congratulating children but from the competencies they acquire. Indeed, being able to accomplish a task provides satisfaction at a much higher level than that of an external acknowledgment by others. Participating in tasks generates in children a sense of sharing and a spirit of helping while also giving them some control over the environment.

Working out a system of task distribution is a good way to introduce the small chores inherent to group life. Pairing children with tasks can be done either on a voluntary basis or by creating a chore board—or it can be determined by chance. See Figure 2.3.

2.12 Offering choices

Democratic pedagogy advocates giving choices to children. The goal is to get children to select a task, or part of it, from among several. A chore poster, a new proposal, or a list of alternatives may help children undertake routine and transition activities. "What task would you like, Lee-Ann?" "It is time to wash hands, Cody. How would you like to go to the sink?" "To get dressed, what would you like to put on first, Jason?"

Cooperation increases when children are convinced they have a place and a say in the activities. A two-year-old may very well have difficulty submitting to established rules and tolerating constraints, but one way to gain his cooperation is to give him choices, even if minimal. "Would you like to sit down by yourself, or would you like some help?" "Would you like to drink your milk before or after your dessert?" With older children, educators may ask open questions crafted to solve

FIGURE 2.3 **Example of tasks for a three-year-old**

My Tasks			
Help educator (picture or photograph) *Name of child*	**Conduct train** (picture or photograph) *Name of child*	**Sweep floor** (picture or photograph) *Name of child*	**Wash table** (picture or photograph) *Name of child*
Hold door (picture or photograph) *Name of child*	**Switch lights off** (picture or photograph) *Name of child*	**Distribute dishes** (picture or photograph) *Name of child*	**Distribute utensils** (picture or photograph) *Name of child*

problems. "What do you think you could do to get outside at the same time as everybody else?"

Be careful not to offer any false choices to children. "Could you please get dressed?" is ineffective since the child does not really have a choice whether or not to get dressed. To avoid ambiguity, issue clear requests with a firm and calm voice. "It is time to get dressed." "You must get dressed now."

2.13 Ensuring consistency

To ensure a smooth flow of activities, it is necessary to keep the directions the same from one time to the next and to respect the various stages of a routine. This way, children know what to expect, they feel secure, they cooperate, they are ready to perform their given tasks, and they learn better. This is especially true of younger children, who desperately need stability and to be able to predict what will happen next. Older children, on the other hand, may be given more flexibility, depending on the situation. Observing the children will show the educator which course to take.

2.14 Building a game bank

All educators have a stockpile of activities they fall back on. However, activities that can be done during routines and transitions may not be as well known, and the ones we tend to depend on are sometimes outmoded or insufficient to the task at hand, which is to hold children's attention. Some tricks may transform a simple idea into an interesting activity, and may even add excitement to a "chore" like personal hygiene. (You can never have enough of these tricks on hand.) There is no magic formula when working with children, but routines and transitions can be transformed into enjoyable and teachable moments by playing certain games. Several suggestions for renewing or refreshing existing strategies are listed throughout the rest of this book.

Educators can profit from developing, through the years, a large bank of games for any situation. An educational toolbox or several theme boxes filled with various objects and accessories may be used to spark games and brighten routine and transition periods. Store ideas and tricks for games in a fil-ing cabinet or a binder so they are on hand when needed. Notes on children's preferences and motivations may help in tailoring these games to specific situations. Substitute educators will also benefit from having access to such a reference.

2.15 Planning the end of activities

When scheduling activities, it is best to leave five to ten minutes to wind down and announce the end of an activity and what will occur next. "This is the time to tidy up so that we can play outside before lunch." The end of an activity may be announced by a sound clue, such as a song, a small bell, a little music box, or a timer with a pleasant ringer. It can also be announced by a visual clue, such as a banner swayed around the room. Take advantage of the situation to introduce the transition: "I wonder if the swallows we saw yesterday are still outside in the tree. Let's go and see. However, before we go outside, we need to get dressed." Or ask children to recognize what is coming by a question: "What do we usually do after gym?" Reminding the children who know how to tell time to look at the clock helps them take some initiative.

A poster with pictures or drawings illustrating the different periods of the schedule can help children anticipate activities. "Look at the poster, Devora. You can see what must be done when you finish your drawing." (Tidy up the materials, and choose another activity.)

2.16 Considering children in context

It is important to keep expectations realistic, reasonable, and within the parameters of child development. Expectations also must reflect the children's previous experiences and be tailored to their physical and mental predispositions as well as to their life context. Educators are responsible for understanding the mental development of children, their memory, their attention, and their personality. Such understanding is particularly useful when attempting to introduce a child to new types of behavior or new skills. For example, children who are new in a group will probably have difficulty falling asleep during naptime. They will need help to acquire this new habit. At the same time, the expectations for children who just turned three are not the same as for those who are almost four. For example, when getting dressed, older children need fewer repetitions of verbal directions than younger ones and can be expected to get dressed faster. Also, remember that special events such as holidays or a long weekend are sure to generate stress in children. During these times, educators must show more tolerance for disruptive behaviors.

Early childhood educators must also deal with numerous extraneous factors. These may include a bilingual or multilingual environment, the size of the center (large or small), homogeneous (for example, kindergarten only) or heterogeneous groups, children with special needs (children with Down's syndrome, hemophilia, diabetes, hyperactivity, and so forth), and board and governmental requirements. Clearly, educators are constantly required to adapt and to be resourceful.

2.17 Analyzing successes and difficulties

Educators must constantly analyze the actions taken when problems arise. The time to stop and think about problematic situations is precisely when nothing seems to be working. Sometimes, the solutions are easy: start lunch fifteen minutes earlier, have children get up in stages after nap, and so forth. Preschool children may sometimes find their own solutions. Why not ask them? They usually have good ideas, and they will feel involved in solving the problem.

One problematic situation is the bathroom routine. We will analyze it here and suggest solutions based upon this analysis. This example considers a large group of four- and five-year-old children in a child care center. See Table 2.1.

There are several factors to consider within this analysis:

- When to implement a new strategy (avoid the day before a weekend or a holiday when introducing a new procedure).
- Your own personal state (when tired, it is better to stick to a known routine).
- The children's mood (such as a high level of excitement at the first snowfall).
- The children's previous experience with the approach to the solution (for example, since children like singing, incorporating this into a solution is often successful).
- The rhythm of the activity (too slow, too fast, or rushed).
- The level of difficulty (solutions that are too easy or too difficult may discourage children).
- Children's interest in the theme (for example, if they can be made a part of the solution, dinosaurs or jungle animals are always sure to interest four-year-olds).
- Children's habits (for example, using role play the first time children are asked to move from one area to another).

It is especially important to take a fresh look at the established methods, procedures, and ways of any early childhood education program. Habit may be the only reason some practices are still in use, and the underlying reasons for them may no longer be valid. However, introducing any kind of modification may be quite taxing. Like everyone else, educators prefer to keep their old routines in place and will readily invent reasons to reject change: fear of the unknown, lack of motivation and knowledge, lack of solidarity within the team, lack of time to discuss the problem, and so forth. A thousand reasons are always offered to sabotage initiatives for change. Here are examples of such excuses:

- "This is impossible to do!"
- "It won't work, I am convinced!"
- "We never did this before!"
- "I have no time for that!"
- "It is way too complicated!"
- "We will do it another year!"
- "Why go through the trouble? Nobody will appreciate it!"
- "I'll believe it when I see it."

2.18 Giving clear verbal directions

As stated before, adults often ask children if they would like to do things when, in fact, they do not have a choice. "Would you like to put away the toys?" "Could you please calm down?" These are false questions. We do not really want to give children a choice, and we cannot afford to have the request rejected. Do not hesitate to politely use the imperative form to clearly formulate a request. "Abigail, please put away the truck." "I would like you to calm down." A calm and convincing tone of voice is effective when asking children to do something.

A positive way of phrasing requests has the advantage of stressing the expected behaviors and minimizing the negative aspects. The best way to make yourself understood is to tell children what they have to do instead of telling them what not to do. To clarify a request, replace "Don't do this!" with "Leave the food on your plate, or put it in your mouth!"

Another way to ensure compliance is to use simple and concise language adapted to the children's level of understanding. A two-year-old will not understand a request to speak more softly if she is told, "Please lower the volume of your voice" or "Your voice is too loud." Also, when asking her to speak softly, it is more effective to give her a good example of this at the same time. Likewise, the request made to a preschool child to behave like a big person may be clear for an adult but ambiguous for the child. What does it

TABLE 2.1 **Analysis of a problematic situation with four- and five-year-olds in a child care center**

Situation	Behaviors observed	Proposed strategies	Result
Between outdoor play and lunch, two groups of children (nineteen in all) gather to go back inside. They need to use the bathroom and wash their hands. They wait in a single line.	Children start to push and shove each other. Some children show signs of impatience (normal at this time since they are hungry). Some children tease and grab others. A simple joke turns into mockery, and one child starts crying. Educators raise their voices to get the children to calm down.	Have children enter the building gradually. One educator supervises the changing area and the bathroom, while the other supervises the children left outside. One by one, the children who have finished their bathroom routine choose a book and sit down at the table.	Fewer children crowd the changing area, and there is less pushing and shoving. Minimization of passive waiting also minimizes the chances of disorganization. With fewer children to supervise, educators are able to give more individual attention and less disciplinary action. The atmosphere is more relaxed.

mean exactly to behave like a grown-up? Play quietly? Take care of the play material? Stay within the yard limits? It is better to word the request in clear terms that are familiar to the child: positive, specific, and of course, issued with a calm voice. "I want you to take a toy that you like and stay in the yard." "Hold your glass with two hands." Choosing words exempt from ambiguity is an art. For example, "Sit down on your bottom" is more easily understood by an eighteen-month-old child than "I've already told you ten times to sit down properly. I am tired of repeating the same thing." Even with older children, the sentence "Well, a good cleanup is in order" may not clearly convey the message that children have to start to pick up their toys. Remember: clear requests are essential to gaining children's cooperation.

Another technique is to ask a volunteer to pass the message to the other children. Children may sometimes find a better way to get the message through to their peers. Group life often leads children to remind each other of the rules. An example overheard: "We are not allowed to climb on chairs. It is dangerous."

Avoid, at all costs, humiliating remarks such as "Don't give me this again. . . . Stop your fighting!" or "I am tired of your whining!" It is much more positive to tell children what we expect of them in clear and respectful terms.

2.19 Modulating your voice

Different tones of voice surprise children and gain their attention. Why not speak like a little mouse or a robot, or imitate voices heard on TV shows? This technique has the advantage of being usable at all times. Children enjoy hearing adults play with their voices. They perceive it as music, as a pleasurable game.

A calm attitude and a firm and convincing tone of voice add a lot to a request. Obviously, screaming at children is the wrong way to ask them to control themselves! A friendly look, a gentle tap on the shoulder, or a tactful but convincing attitude conveys the message that rules are to be respected. Just make sure that the rules are reasonable.

2.20 Taking direct action

It is better to act than to speak endlessly when announcing a new activity or making a new request. An example or a concrete demonstration allows for faster comprehension than a lengthy explanation. It is easier for children to imitate adults than to try to follow directions. An image is worth a thousand words, and so is an action. So speak less, and act more!

2.21 Staying close to the children

Noise is often considered a stress factor in early childhood education programs. For example, during meals or tidy-up time, when decibels often skyrocket, screaming across the room, "Sit down, Max" or "Who needs her lunch warmed up?" is fruitless. By getting closer to children when speaking to them you can minimize the noise that is unavoidable when several children are present. Unlike most other factors, the voice level of educators can be easily modified. As a general rule, do not raise your voice when speaking to children or addressing them from far away. Children should also be encouraged to follow this rule when speaking to each other.

2.22 Using make-believe

Plenty of smiles and laughter are always present in a successful early childhood education program. It is good to break the monotony of routines with a bit of fantasy. Since children naturally like to play, it is easy to introduce routines and transitions with a bit of fun. Playing "restaurant" during snack time helps children to respect meal etiquette (saying please and thank you, eating calmly, sitting straight on one's chair). This is far more interesting than coldly reminding children to behave without providing any other motivation. Helping children have a fun time using make-believe is an art that must be learned. You can use a change of accent (Italian, French, robot voice, nasal voice, and so forth). You can create a character that comes out once in a while. You can bring out a puppet, a special tray with which to serve food, or a special apron. All these tricks are worth the effort.

We've already mentioned that children like to participate in the selection of activities. In this sense, you can invite them to choose a make-believe theme from among those they already know (sometimes with a little help to remind them of the possibilities). "How are we going to act during snack today? Pretend we are in a restaurant as we did the other day?" "Do you remember what we did with the puppet when we brushed our teeth?" A message is carried so much better with make-believe and fantasy. "I would like to hear some silent shoes when we walk to the changing area to put on our coats." "Place your magic finger on your mouth to walk along the hall." "We are going to walk like detectives trying to find some clues."

Other examples of incorporating make-believe into requests include: "I am going to put on my bionic glasses to check those who are flushing the toilet after use." "Who can park their truck in the garage?" "I am calling all experts in hand washing to the sink!"

> *Children find even the simplest tasks enjoyable when they are involved in fantasy or make-believe.*

2.23 Avoiding the expectation of perfection at all costs

It is unrealistic to believe that we can control all child behavior, however hard we try. As educators, we need to ask ourselves whether our requests are really useful for the development of the children or whether they are merely an expression of a more personal need for control. For instance, enforcing total silence during a walk down the hall is probably not necessary to the successful management of this routine. It is much more realistic to implement some means of motivating the children to calmly cooperate than to force absolute perfection.

2.24 Getting the children's attention

Ensure that you have children's full attention before you give them any information. You can say something like, "I want to have all eyes here," or, in a mysterious voice, "I have something important to tell you. Come here, ladies and gentlemen!" Calling a child by his name with a pleasant voice gets his attention like nothing else. "I need Ali's ears to be wide open before we start the activity." The latest research on the brain shows that the more parts of the brain a message mobilizes, the more it imprints. Images, different tones of voice, and facial expressions stimulate different areas of the brain and provide for additional anchors to the verbal request.

> *Young children need to be reminded to look at you as well as listen to what you say: "I need to see all eyes here." Children listen better if sight is associated with the message. Once you have their visual attention, quickly proceed with an interesting message for them.*

When you want children to listen to directions, why not, once in a while, use a clown nose, a magic wand, a small bell, or a strange hat to motivate them to listen? Remember, you'll get a child's attention better if you gently tap his shoulder as you speak to him and look at him.

2.25 Using positive reinforcement

What child does not like to have her positive behavior noticed? "Bravo!" "Good!" "Wonderful!" "Great!" However, this should be done without dishing out compliments that are out of proportion with the behavior in question and without making automatic remarks. A smile or a hand on the shoulder is a suitable encouragement that helps the child increase her self-esteem and continue her efforts. A simple gesture can be a wordless way of saying, "You have finished all of it. You put a lot of effort into it."

Positive reinforcement is a natural phenomenon, and children's behaviors are part of it (Bredekamp and Copple 1997). Telling children that we appreciate their appropriate behavior is an effective way to implement positive reinforcement. "I am happy to see you tidy up with the others." "I like it when we speak softly during snack time." Moreover, children are impressed when they hear their names mentioned, and that in itself can be positive reinforcement. "Matthew, I can see that you know how to store the trucks." "Wow! Kellen, you heard my request." By addressing children directly, they feel more involved than if the comments are geared to the whole group.

Thanking children is definitely positive reinforcement, characteristic of a well-meaning adult (Miller 1990). "Thank you for cleaning the paintbrushes. They look new!" On the other hand, negative criticism paralyzes children's motivation. "You haven't put away your toys yet. How do you expect me to treat you like a big kid if you don't do things?" Avoid scolding children and distributing punishment according to your own mood. Try to follow just and constant rules.

> *Systematically isolating a child for inappropriate behavior should be avoided. To have a child reflect upon his or her behavior is not always a realistic and effective means to induce a more appropriate behavior. Rather, carefully evaluate the need for such action by considering the age and the event.*

Most educators are keen to humanely implement guidance. They are careful to motivate children with kind words and by smiling and looking at children in a friendly way. Moreover, most educators will carefully act in a coherent and congruent way with their guidance techniques. For instance, if children are allowed to eat and drink only at the table, educators should abstain from drinking coffee while moving around the room. If an educator has to stand on a chair to post a drawing, she should explain to the children why she is breaking the rule of not climbing on chairs at that particular moment.

In some contexts, it is valuable to add privileges to verbal reinforcement. Privileges could include a first turn at the computer, leading the group in a game, or being allowed to bring a video home. Care should be taken when using this technique, however. Its indiscriminate use is discouraged because the positive reinforcement system of earning stickers, posting the name of the child, and so on is of limited usefulness and provides only short-term solutions. In the context of a democratic pedagogy,

this technique is definitely inadequate. This type of intervention must be integrated into a general guidance plan containing various pedagogical strategies within the realm of democratic pedagogy.

2.26 Refocusing the children

Refocusing may help some children stop their disruptive behavior and calm down. "Antwan, come here and help me take out the cots." In situations in which a child might be inclined to be stubborn, hesitant to obey, or unwilling to comply with a request, it is useful to offer him some alternate solutions. "Would you like me to take out your cot, or would you prefer to do it by yourself?" Whenever possible, it is better to ignore a child who creates a disturbance and to focus instead on his efforts related to the task at hand. Avoid trying to persuade him or preach to him. It is generally more effective to ask a question. "What do you have to do now?" Leave the child some time to react and to get interested in the next activity. "When you are through with this, I will need your agile fingers to place the crayons in their box."

2.27 Encouraging individual thinking

It is always tempting to issue orders, since many situations lend themselves to this. "Be quiet! Sit down and stay there." "Go back to your place." "Stop running." "Wash your hands now." Such commands appear to have an immediate effect. However, they suppress all independent thinking. A child's development will be enhanced whenever she is led to think. Asking children open questions will help them to remember the usual rules. "What do you need to do after using the toilet?" "Look at the board to see what you could be doing now. Are you allowed to do this?" Democratic pedagogy is meant to help children develop their thinking abilities. "Look. Check the poster on the wall." "Listen carefully." "Think about it carefully." "How will you zip up your coat if you are putting your mittens on right away?"

In summary, children will be much more cooperative if educators take the time to use guidance techniques that help their overall development.

2.28 Showing perseverance and optimism

What educator has not been tempted to abandon her goal when faced with a stubborn child? It is not easy to accept that a two-year-old is opposing any change in a routine or a transition or is indifferent to it. In such cases you need to persevere so that children will be able to master the changes, to get from the known to the unknown. If children are used to rushing to the sink, they might find it difficult to wash their hands one by one. Remember not to abandon a new idea right away if it is not successful. Children will overcome their resistance and learn the new routine if given the time to do so. Your optimism and perseverance will surely encourage children's participation.

2.29 Showing flexibility

Allowing a child to watch when he doesn't want to become involved in the play of others can be just as beneficial in terms of his learning as actual playing might have been. For instance, observing other children singing can help a child memorize the lyrics. It is important to remain flexible within the framework of democratic pedagogy.

2.30 Ensuring the well-being of educators

Although children should remain the main concern in an early childhood education program, the health and safety of the staff should also be a priority. Since they spend a long time leading routine and transition activities, early childhood educators are entitled to adequate physical settings and equipment. They must have good working conditions that allow them to accomplish tasks successfully and efficiently. The following should be included: an adult chair, an ergonomic seat for sitting on the floor, carts to move materials around, windows that open easily to air the room after snacks, adequate and regular breaks, a well-equipped staff room reserved for staff members, adequate pedagogical support from the administrators, free training workshops, paid preparation/planning periods, and paid meeting time for staff meetings or parent/caregiver meetings. Don't forget that adult-sized furniture must also be child-safe (Pimento and Kernested 2004).

Because it has a direct influence on their well-being, educators need to assess the way they do things, trying to avoid postures and movements harmful for the back, negative attitudes toward parents/caregivers, work habits leading to professional burnout, withdrawal from the work team, and so forth.

When educators feel appreciated in their work environment, they are more inclined to accomplish their professional duties to the best of their abilities. The more they are motivated, the more they want to contribute to children's development. Do not forget, however, that educators are themselves the best ones to recognize, praise, and improve their profession. They are contributing to their own professional well-being by getting quality education, by regularly showcasing their work, by participating in the improvement of their working conditions, by developing the ability to self-evaluate, and by managing their stress. Contributing to their professionalism also means adopting and following coherent policies and ethical codes.

3

Hygiene

CHAPTER CONTENTS

3.1 Hand washing
    A. Materials and equipment
    B. When to wash hands
    C. Hand-washing techniques
    D. Setting a good example
    E. Hand-washing training
    F. Games
    G. Songs
3.2 Toothbrushing
    A. When to brush teeth
    B. Materials and equipment
    C. Toothbrushing techniques
    D. Games and tricks

3.3 Bathroom routine
    A. Bathroom use
    B. Diaper changing
    C. Hygiene and sanitation
    D. Saying the right thing at the
       right time
3.4 Nose blowing
    A. When to blow noses
    B. Materials and equipment
    C. Nose-blowing techniques

Personal hygiene plays an important role in children's physical health. Activities that foster hygiene help reinforce the immune system, which is immature during the first years of life.

This chapter covers hand washing, toothbrushing, bathroom routines, and nose blowing, and addresses why hygiene routines are essential to the prevention of infectious diseases such as gastroenteritis, colds, and conjunctivitis.

3.1 Hand washing

Hand washing is the single best means of preventing infections from bacteria, viruses, and parasites. These microorganisms can be directly or indirectly transmitted by people and objects. Epidemiological research has shown that hands are the main source of transmission of infections (Pimento and Kernested 2004). Hand washing needs to be taken seriously because it reduces these risks by up to 50 percent. Moreover, hand washing is a concrete way to foster children's well-being by decreasing diseases caused by contamination.

Effective hand washing is a health habit children need for the rest of their lives (Pimento and Kernested 2004). Early childhood educators have to pay special attention to the hand washing of young children, whose immune systems are still immature.

> The important role educators play in preventing diseases and keeping children healthy cannot be stressed enough. Children acquire good personal hygiene practices with the help of adults. In particular, they can learn when and how to wash their hands.

A. MATERIALS AND EQUIPMENT

Sinks should be at a child's height and located where children take their meals. Another option is to install sinks at regular height and use movable antiskid steps for children. This option has the advantage of sparing the educator's back. Another point to consider is the use of separate sinks for hand washing, food handling, and toilet routines. (Check your local health codes.) A sink with a handless faucet or single faucet is easier for children to use.

Liquid soap in a dispenser is easier to handle than a bar and more hygienic as well. Soap bars may transmit microorganisms since people touch the bars with dirty hands. The use of germicidal soap should be avoided as much as possible because of its irritating effect. Such soaps also contribute to the increased resistance of bacteria. Limit their use to when an epidemic strikes (colds, gastroenteritis, chicken pox). Soap distributors should be equipped with a disposable soap container, or the containers must be washed before refilling. Hands should be dried with disposable paper towels to avoid contamination. Cloth towels can transmit germs from one person to another. However, check that children do not overuse paper towels so as to limit waste and pollution. Electric hand dryers aren't recommended because they can break and they take a long time to dry the hands. Only in exceptional situations, where sinks are not available, should a sanitizing hand solution without a rinse or wipes be used. These products are more expensive than soap.

A garbage can lined with a plastic bag must be placed next to each sink to dispose of used paper towels, to discourage young children from throwing them in the toilet. Ideally, a lidded step can should be used to avoid hand contact with the cover. (Garbage can covers are heavily contaminated by wastes such as food, dirty diapers, and soiled paper towels.) All garbage cans—indoor and outdoor—must be sanitized regularly (check your local regulations for frequency). Use a solution of one part bleach to nine parts water as a sanitizer.

The following method can be used for very young children who are unable to access a sink: squirt a small amount of soap on one corner of a wet face cloth, wash the child's hands, and rinse the hands with the other corner of the face cloth. Remember, though, that nothing can replace a thorough hand washing at the sink with warm water. Other methods, such as wet paper towels or face cloths, wipes, and sanitizing hand solutions, should be used only in emergency situations.

B. WHEN TO WASH HANDS

Appropriate hand washing with warm water and soap is not enough. It also has to be done at the right time to maximize its efficiency. These rules should be followed by educators as well as children. See Box 3.1.

BOX 3.1 **When to wash hands (from the NAEYC Accreditation Criteria for Health Standards)**

The program follows these practices regarding hand washing:

- Staff members and those children who are developmentally able to learn personal hygiene are taught hand-washing procedures and are periodically monitored.

- Hand washing is required by all staff, volunteers, and children when hand washing would reduce the risk of transmission of infectious diseases to themselves and to others.

- Staff assist children with hand washing as needed to successfully complete the task. Children wash either independently or with staff assistance.

Children and adults wash their hands:

- on arrival for the day;

- after diapering or using the toilet (use of wet wipes is acceptable for infants);

- after handling body fluids (e.g., blowing or wiping a nose, coughing on a hand, or touching any mucus, blood, or vomit);

- before meals and snacks, before preparing or serving food, or after handling any raw food that requires cooking (e.g., meat, eggs, poultry);

- after playing in water that is shared by two or more people;

- after handling pets and other animals or any materials such as sand, dirt, or surfaces that might be contaminated by contact with animals; and

- when moving from one group to another (e.g., visiting) that involves contact with infants and toddlers/twos.

Adults also wash their hands:

- before and after feeding a child;

- before and after administering medication;

- after assisting a child with toileting; and

- after handling garbage or cleaning.

Proper hand-washing procedures are followed by adults and children and include:

- using liquid soap and running water;

- rubbing hands vigorously for at least 10 seconds, including back of hands, wrists, between fingers, under and around any jewelry, and under fingernails;

- rinsing well;

- drying hands with a paper towel, a single-use towel, or a dryer; and

- avoiding touching the faucet with just-washed hands (e.g., by using a paper towel to turn off water).

Except when handling blood or body fluids that might contain blood (when wearing gloves is required), wearing gloves is an optional supplement, but not a substitute, for hand washing in any required hand-washing situation listed above.

- Staff wear gloves when contamination with blood may occur.

- Staff do not use hand-washing sinks for bathing children or for removing smeared fecal material.

- In situations where sinks are used for both food preparation and other purposes, staff clean and sanitize the sinks before using them to prepare food.

Note: The use of alcohol-based hand rubs in lieu of hand washing is not recommended for early education and child care settings. If these products are used as a temporary measure, a sufficient amount must be used to keep hands wet for 15 seconds. Since the alcohol-based hand rubs are toxic and flammable, they must be stored and used according to the manufacturer's instructions.

C. HAND-WASHING TECHNIQUE

There is more to hand washing than using water and soap. Box 3.2 describes the proper way to wash hands.

BOX 3.2 **Proper hand-washing technique**

- Remove rings, watch, bracelets.
- Turn up sleeves to bare the forearms.
- Open faucet to get warm water (avoid scalding). To conserve water, don't turn on the tap full blast.
- Wet hands under running water. Wetting hands before applying soap reduces skin dryness.
- Squirt a little bit of soap from soap dispenser.
- Rub hands for about 15 seconds (30–45 seconds if hands are visibly dirty). Remember to include palm and back of hands, finger tips, spaces between fingers, and wrists.
- Rinse well by rubbing hands under running water.
- Dry hands with disposable paper towel without rubbing to avoid chafing.
- Close faucet with used paper towel.
- Throw paper towel in garbage can without touching can with hands.

Time used for washing hands is time well spent because it minimizes the risk of disease. Ask parents to regularly cut their children's nails, since the spaces under the nails harbor germs. And remember to keep your own nails short!

D. SETTING A GOOD EXAMPLE

It is important for the educator to wash her hands in front of children to set a good example: after using the toilet, before and after touching food, after helping to blow a nose, after changing a diaper, and after touching a soiled object or a cleaning product. Children learn by observing adults, especially significant adults. They more easily accept the need to do certain things when those things are consistent with an adult's actions. Stress that

you also wash your hands and that this is a good habit for adults as well as for children. "See, I also wash my hands before eating because I care about my health."

E. HAND-WASHING TRAINING

Good hand-washing technique fosters the development of fine-motor skills, hand coordination, body image, and memory in children. It also teaches children to take care of their health. Around fifteen to eighteen months, toddlers are usually ready to learn about washing their hands at the sink. However, it is not until the age of four that children are finally able to wash their hands efficiently. Before that, regular reminders and close supervision will be necessary to show them how to lather their hands all over, and so forth.

Remind children why hand washing is important (how it reduces colds and diarrhea within the group). Simple explanations are the best. "When you wash your hands, you will stop the germs that may make you sick."

Some children may even enjoy spending time playing with soap and water. If necessary, redirect children's attention. For instance, you may ask children to contribute by performing small tasks: distributing paper towels, turning off faucets, checking to see if the other children's hands smell good, thinking of the next activity, and so forth.

A well-placed poster or a video about hand washing shown at regular intervals will reinforce the fact that hand washing is important. You may also introduce creative ideas to encourage children to take care of themselves. The following activity encourages children to wash their hands with warm water and soap and demonstrates the

presence of germs that are invisible to the naked eye: Put a very small amount of petroleum jelly in the palm of each child's hand. Ask them to rub their hands. Then ask them to wash their hands under cold water, without soap. Show them that the water glides off the hands and that the "germs" do not go away. Repeat the hand washing with warm water. This time only a little bit of the petroleum jelly goes away. Repeat the hand washing the proper way: use warm water, soap, and lots of lather, then rinse thoroughly. This time, the "germs" are all gone. Conclude: "Good hand washing is something that needs to be done with warm water and soap."

F. GAMES

Hand washing is done about ten times a day, for a total of two thousand times a year for each child in a child care setting! To break the monotony of this activity, educators can organize games to introduce variety into this routine.

> *A little stroke of a magic wand, as well as humor, spontaneity, and pleasure, makes the monotony of hand washing disappear.*

Indeed, with good planning, positive attitudes, a few simple ideas, and a little fun, hand washing can become quite interesting. Games allow children to associate pleasure with routine actions and minimize negative interventions by educators. Box 3.3 includes suggestions to use before or during the routine.

BOX 3.3 **Suggestions to motivate children to wash their hands**

- With toddlers, talk with them about what they are doing as they are doing it, making comments like "The water is warm" or "The cloth feels soft and wet" (Pimento and Kernested 2004).

- Go to the sink using an unusual walk: small steps like a mouse, walking on heels, walking on tiptoes, and so forth. Use the theme of the moment and the children's interests to get ideas.

- Go to the sink with an added challenge: walk with hands on heads, along an imaginary line, on a line drawn with masking tape, or around a chair.

- Draw out of a box or hat the name of the next child to wash hands, or call a child according to specific characteristics. "I am calling the child wearing a blue sweater with a design."

- Once in a while, initiate a conversation among children about hygiene to introduce the idea of taking care of their bodies. A book on the subject may introduce the discussion.

- Organize a relay game to get to the sink, having the children exchange an object or a password.

- Use a puppet to supervise hand washing and to remind the children of the rules.

- Try a fruity soap if there are no allergies to it. Children especially like fruity fragrances such as green apple, strawberry, mandarin, or grape.

- Allow children to apply some hypoallergenic hand lotion after hand washing. For children who have severe skin allergies, sunblock lotion provided by the parents could be used.

- Give children some special "clean hand boxes." These boxes can be used only with clean hands. They contain several types of objects: Small puzzles, little figures, paper and pencil, mittens, and so forth.

G. SONGS

Even though the skill of washing hands and singing simultaneously is perfected only around age five or six, younger children are motivated by hearing songs and nursery rhymes about what to do. These songs also remind them of the hand-washing steps and actions. Popular children's songs can be modified to include words about hand washing. Here is an example to the tune of "Here We Go 'Round the Mulberry Bush."

This the way we wash our hands,
Wash our hands, wash our hands.
This is the way we wash our hands
Before [or after] every meal.

3.2 Toothbrushing

Tooth decay is still a problem in modern society. During childhood, it is crucial to acquire good dental hygiene habits.

Primary teeth are not just the precursors of adult teeth. They also play a major role in enunciation, chewing, and digestion, so they need to stay healthy and in place until the permanent teeth grow, between the ages of six and eleven years.

> *Young children need to be introduced to healthy food, and the consumption of food with a high content of refined sugar needs to be reduced, especially between meals. Children should also learn how to brush their teeth as soon as possible after eating.*

Good teeth and healthy gums in childhood prevent the premature loss of teeth, as well as language problems and problems caused by poor dental occlusion (bite). Last, but not least, good dental hygiene minimizes pain caused by tooth decay, dental extractions, and repairs that are often psychologically difficult for children. It also reduces the costs of dental care! Since teeth play an important role in children's overall health, it is vital that adults take children's dental health seriously.

If you need further convincing of the necessity of keeping a toothbrushing routine front and center, remember that many children are left to brush their teeth on their own at home and that half of all children will have tooth decay before they start school.

Unfortunately, some centers have abolished toothbrushing because of a fear of transmitting hepatitis B or HIV. However, some precautions will control the risk of contamination that is, in fact, very minimal in the first place. Those precautions include wall toothbrush stands, which allow the toothbrushes to air dry, and supervision, so that children do not exchange their toothbrushes with each other.

A daily toothbrushing routine is recommended, even if it takes time. At the center, the best time to brush teeth is after lunch. If children brush their teeth in the morning and at night at home, they will be further motivated by such a practice. The benefits in terms of the prevention of tooth decay far exceed the inconveniences. For educational purposes, if a daily toothbrushing routine is impossible, it should at least be enforced two or three times a week, or on a rotating basis.

A. WHEN TO BRUSH TEETH

For infants who have no teeth yet, it is a good idea to clean the gums and the inside of the mouth with a wet cloth to introduce them to good dental hygiene habits. Toothbrushing with a toothbrush can start with children older than one year who receive two or more meals (NAEYC Accreditation Criteria). For children in an early childhood program, a closely supervised toothbrushing should take place after lunch or before nap. Since toothbrushing should be done at least twice a day, parents should have children brush their teeth at bedtime. This is the best time to minimize dental plaque.

B. MATERIALS AND EQUIPMENT

Obviously, a toothbrush is the main tool of good dental hygiene. Parents are responsible for providing a small toothbrush with a waterproof label bearing the name of the child. Ask them to choose a toothbrush with a small head, soft bristles, and an easy-grip rubber handle. Toothbrushes must be changed at least two or three times a year, when bristles look bent or are damaged, or when they are coated with toothpaste (and bacteria!). They must be replaced rather than disinfected. When an epidemic strikes, old toothbrushes must be replaced immediately with new ones.

To prevent bacterial contamination, toothbrushes must be stored in a sanitary way after each use. The bristles should be air dried and at the same time be protected from dust. A stand should be used that allows toothbrushes to hang in a way that prevents any contact among them. They shouldn't drip on one another. Acrylic stands that meet these criteria are available for purchase. These stands must be easily removable, since they must be washed regularly.

> *Once a week, toothbrush stands must be washed and soaked in a sanitizing solution for two or three minutes before being rinsed thoroughly. During episodes of gastroenteritis, colds, or contagious diseases, they must be washed more often.*

Protective caps or cases that allow air into them (so that the bristles will dry) should be used to protect the individual brushes. It is important that the casing around the bristles allows air in; bacteria thrive in a humid environment and will certainly grow on the bristles if air is blocked. It is essential to sanitize protective caps or cases every week to reduce the risk of contamination.

Educators must supervise toothbrushing. This includes giving children clear guidelines prohibiting exchanges or loans of toothbrushes, which lead to germ transfer. If an exchange occurs, or one toothbrush touches another, both toothbrushes must be replaced.

> *Remember, close supervision is essential to sanitary toothbrushing. It is best to supervise one child at a time.*

Toothpaste is optional, especially fluoride toothpaste, with very young children who may not be able to spit thoroughly.

C. TOOTHBRUSHING TECHNIQUES

Although there is no consensus among specialists on the proper way to brush teeth, there are some essential guidelines. For children two- and three-years-old, limit the number of guidelines to three so they don't get discouraged. Ask them to take the brush by the handle so they do not contaminate the bristles with their hands. Suggest a little game, such as stroking or tickling each tooth with their toothbrush while leaving their mouth open.

Remember that children's fine-motor development does not allow them to brush teeth efficiently before the age of six. This means that educators, as well as parents, must finish the job for children to ensure teeth are properly brushed. Place yourself behind the child to help him perform the correct motions.

Preschool children can learn a few precise motions. They can learn to keep their mouths open and to brush the outer surface of their teeth in the direction of tooth growth, which means from the top to the bottom for the upper teeth and from the bottom to the top for the lower teeth. The motion must start from the gum line. For the inner surface, the teeth must be brushed with horizontal stokes. Calculate five strokes for each tooth segment. A complete brushing takes about two minutes for each child.

Children become efficient at flossing only around age ten or eleven, so parents have to start flossing their children's teeth for them at home, preferably before the evening toothbrushing, and especially in areas that are difficult to reach with a toothbrush. Proper dental hygiene also requires regular visits to the dentist, ideally twice a year.

Since children enjoy imitating adults, you can set a good example by brushing your teeth in front of them. Remember that this is one of the best ways for them to acquire good dental hygiene habits. Also, children should not be fed pureed or ground food for too long because chewing and salivation help to eliminate waste from the surface of teeth.

D. GAMES AND TRICKS

- Give a shatterproof mirror to children so they can check that their teeth are well brushed.

- Use a toothbrushing puppet to promote and check toothbrushing. The puppet can have a funny name and voice.

- Role-play dentists and dental hygienists examining brushed teeth.

- Give children a little notebook or calendar where they can draw a smiling tooth after they have finished brushing their teeth.

- Use a visual prop such as a giant cardboard toothbrush to remind children of tooth-brushing time.

- Add a safe decoration on the toothbrush handle: a ribbon or a tip made of air-hardened clay.

- Plan a visit to a dental hygienist or invite one to the center. Some dental clinics or dental hygienist associations offer this service at no charge. Colleges that offer a dental hygiene course may also be good resources.

3.3 Bathroom routine

Most preschool children are able to use the toilet alone when they feel the need for it. They are able to recognize the signs of a need for elimination. However, some children restrain themselves because they are too busy or because they do not want to disturb the group in the middle of an activ-ity. In this case, you will observe children wiggle, touch their genitals, crouch, or isolate themselves. A quiet reminder will guide them to the bathroom. "I think you need to go to the bathroom now. You will feel better afterward."

For beginners a closer supervision of this routine is necessary. Two- and three-year-old children need some regularity to help them structure their time. They should use the bathroom before going outside, before nap, and before the drive home. You might have to teach them not to take off all their clothes when using the potty or the adapted toilet seat. You must regularly check to see if children need to go to the bathroom, based on your observations of them. "Do you need to go to the bathroom?" "Do you have a pee coming?" "Maybe your little farts tell you that a poop wants to come out."

A. BATHROOM USE

Child-size toilets for two- to six-year-olds are a big help. If this is not possible, adapted seats on regular toilets are a must. Potties, adapted seats, or child-size toilets must be comfortable, very stable, and easy to clean and sanitize.

It is also helpful to plan a bathroom for educators close to the main room.

Most centers use the same bathrooms for boys and girls. Before the age of six, mixed bathrooms allow children to consider their sexual differences as normal (Hendrick 1988). Open toilets have the advantage of allowing children to satisfy their curiosity. Some bathrooms are equipped with stalls without doors. However, remember that some children may have a legitimate need for privacy for religious or family reasons. Just think of our uneasiness, as adults, if we have to use a bathroom without a door.

> Children should always be able to choose between an open stall and a closed one without having to justify their choice. Educators must always be available to help a child wipe and pull up underpants and pants if needed.

In exceptional situations, when a child feels an urgent need to use the bathroom but has to wait her turn, simple games can help her wait calmly. This will minimize the tension generated by groups and inactivity. (See chapter 11 for information on unavoidable waiting periods.)

Easy access to a bathroom from the outside play area will greatly facilitate bathroom time. It is also helpful if pants are easy to take off, with an elastic waistband and no complex buttons or belt. You might find it necessary to ask parents to dress their children in easy-to-remove clothes.

B. DIAPER CHANGING

When diapers are soiled with urine only, it is easier and quicker to change two- and three-year-olds while they stand in place, if they will hold the position. This also minimizes the stress on your back, since you do not need to lift the child onto the changing table. As soon as a child can climb steps, he can use a small step to make the task easier for you. Do not forget to prepare everything you will need before starting to change the diaper. An easy way to plan this is to have a basket on hand containing the supplies for each child. As long as this basket is close by, you will not have a problem. Remember that at all times the child's privacy must be protected.

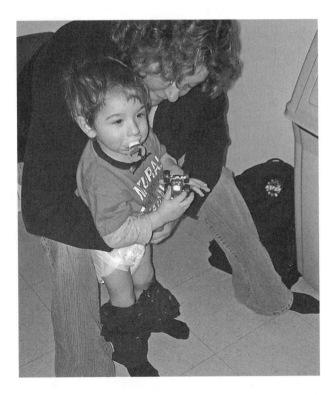

Some basic precautions to limit the spread of germs: wash your hands and the child's hands,

sanitize the changing table, and wear gloves when changing a diaper with a bowel movement. (Check your health codes—you may be required to wear gloves with all diaper changes.)

Diaper changes are privileged times for personal interaction between you and the child. It is important to show an interest in the child and to communicate and establish complicity with the child at this time.

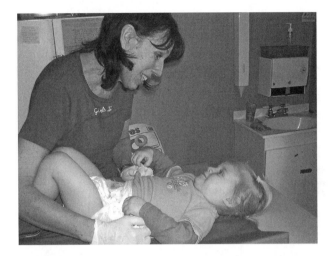

Even outside the normal toilet-training period, children may have accidents. It is essential to ban all negative and humiliating remarks, as well as heavy silences, that only increase the child's uneasiness at such times. Rather, comfort and reassure the child and change her without delay. However, be careful not to convey a tacit approval. If the situation occurs repeatedly without obvious reason, approach the parents and quietly discuss the case. Ensure that the parents provide a change of clothes (socks, pants, underpants) to leave at the center. However, it is always good to have handy a supply of clothes belonging to the center in case a child has no personal change of clothes. To ensure that they are brought back, these clothes should be labeled with the name of the center.

> *Educators who follow a democratic approach know that children's well-being and the development of children's autonomy are the main focuses of their educational actions. They consider toilet training a component of children's overall development, and they will work in collaboration with parents.*

C. HYGIENE AND SANITATION

Children develop sound personal hygiene practices by observing others and by being regularly reminded of the proper procedures. For example, washing hands after using the toilet is far from being a simple reflex action for children younger than eight (or even for adults!). Your responsibility is to introduce these healthy habits using all the means at your disposal, including frequent repetition. Procedures that are important throughout life include using toilet paper correctly (wiping from the front to the back for girls), lifting the toilet seat when boys urinate standing up and then lowering it, flushing the toilet, and washing hands.

Toilets must be sanitized properly each day, and potties and changing tables must be sanitized after each use. An easy-to-clean bathroom floor is a must. The bathroom must also have proper ventilation and lighting, and should include attractive decorations.

D. SAYING THE RIGHT THING AT THE RIGHT TIME

In spite of the inane connotations adults usually give to words such as *pee, wee wee,* and *poop,* young children need to use those simple words to describe their elimination needs. "To go to the bathroom," "to move one's bowels," and "to urinate" are unfamiliar terms to them. Baby talk such as "pee" or "poop" is fine if it is used for the right reason at the right time. "Do you need to pee?" Preschoolers have more modesty and prefer to say they need to go to the bathroom. However, at different times over the course of the day, they are likely to say "pee," "poop," or "butt" for a different reason: they know it is a way to make people react. If the use of scatological terms is a problem, ask children to reserve these terms for bathroom time.

It is only around five or six years of age that children will be at ease hearing and using terms that are more medical in nature to describe their basic functions: to move a bowel, to urinate, to be constipated. "You say your tummy aches? Did you urinate? Do you have diarrhea?"

3.4 Nose blowing

For children less than six years old, blowing the nose is common during several months of the year. During the winter months especially there are colds, earaches, and sinusitis, and in spring and summer there can be seasonal allergic reactions (hay fever, allergies to pollen or grasses). If children are affected by these problems, nose blowing can occur several times a day.

Each time a child sneezes or his nose runs, there is a risk of spreading an infection through nasal secretions. Sneezing in the hands, a runny nose, or fingers in contact with mucus foster rapid germ proliferation for thirty to sixty minutes. However, viruses can be contained with the right actions.

In many cases, children need to be taught how to blow their noses properly. They also need to know how to sneeze when facial tissue is unavailable. In child care centers, educators are responsible for teaching children the proper rules regarding nose blowing. However, since each child's health concerns more than one person, it is essential to follow up with other staff members as well as parents.

A. WHEN TO BLOW NOSES

From two-years-old on, children can generally start learning how to blow their noses (including how and when to do it), but they will only be able to perform this task adequately around four years of age.

There are a few basic rules to observe by children and adults alike when blowing a nose. Nose blowing must happen in the following situations:

- When sneezing.
- When the nose is running profusely.
- When there seems to be some secretion and sniffling occurs repeatedly.
- When the need is felt.
- When nostrils have dry secretion or waste.

B. MATERIALS AND EQUIPMENT

Facial tissue is obviously preferable to cloth handkerchiefs for reasons of hygiene. Facial tissue should be big and thick. It definitely is a single-use item. This means that you cannot use it twice on the same child, or use it on one child and then on another. During all seasons, boxes of facial tissue need to be placed in each room of the center, as well as outside. Facial tissue also should be available during outings to the park and during bus trips.

Educators have to teach children to blow their noses by themselves. Therefore, tissue should be easily accessible whenever needed. Frequently, parents are asked to bring one box of facial tissue for their child. Use one box at a time, and replace it when it is used up. Mounting a wall support for a box of tissues or placing the box at the end of a counter will make it easier to locate.

A garbage can, preferably a step can lined with a plastic bag, should be conveniently located in each room or area where children are. It should be emptied and sanitized daily. For ecological reasons it is better to use facial tissue made of recycled fibers.

C. NOSE-BLOWING TECHNIQUES

First, take one or two tissues, big and thick enough so that the fingers do not come directly into contact with the mucus, and cover the nose and nostrils with hands placed on either side. Second, blow softly, one nostril at a time, while blocking the other nostril with the other hand. This technique prevents the nasal secretions from blowing into the eustachian tube, minimizing the risk of middle ear infections (Larose 2000). Third, throw the tissue in the garbage. Finally, wash hands with warm water and soap.

> *Facial tissue does not constitute an effective barrier between nasal secretion and hands, so it is essential to wash the hands after nose blowing to minimize the risk of spreading germs.*

Inserting fingers in the nostrils may scratch or injure them. Germs may also get caught under the fingernails, which is a good reason to keep children's nails short.

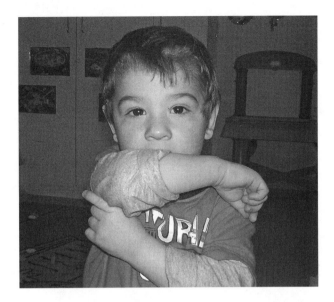

Sneezing is a reflex that often occurs suddenly. There is usually no time to grab a tissue. To diminish the risk of hand contamination and the spread of germs, it is a good idea to teach children to sneeze into the bend of their arm. However, some children abuse this practice and develop the bad habit of regularly wiping their runny nose with their forearm or the bend of their arm. They should be gently reminded to use a tissue, with the explanation that this is a cleaner way to blow their nose and that it will prevent them from getting sick.

Here is a little game to teach beginners how to blow their nose properly:

Draw a little ghost on a piece of facial tissue. Ask the child to blow into the tissue to chase away the ghost, first with her mouth open, then closed. Then place the tissue in front of her nose, and ask the child to try to move the ghost by blowing on it through her nostrils. Finally, block one nostril, and ask the child to blow on the ghost directly through the other nostril.

4

Snacks and Meals

CHAPTER CONTENTS

4.1 Healthy diet

4.2 Children's typical food preferences

4.3 Managing the task of meals and snacks

4.4 Physical and material organization

4.5 Creating a positive mealtime atmosphere

4.6 Mealtimes with two-year-olds

4.7 Lack of appetite, refusal to eat, and other challenges

    A. Eating patterns and children's temperaments

    B. Eating patterns at different ages

    C. Observing children's eating patterns

    D. Individual eating habits

    E. Useful meal and snack strategies

    F. Emotions and eating habits

    G. Food preferences

    H. Fluctuating appetites

4.8 Eating habits and special diets

4.9 Overeating

4.10 Table manners

4.11 Allergies and food intolerance

4.12 Choking dangers

4.13 Nutrition education

    A. Encouraging children's participation during meals

    B. Food awareness

    C. Introducing nutrition throughout the curriculum

        1.) Food theme at circle time

        2.) Food-themed activities

        3.) Materials for dramatic play

        4.) Educational field trips

        5.) Other games

Eating is not just a physical necessity for children, it is also a source of pleasure and well-being; a sensory, social, and emotional activity; and a great opportunity for learning. Educators using democratic pedagogy frame snacks and meals within a continuum of activities in which children have a privileged role. Educators plan and implement snack and meal activities with the same care as any other activity.

Food education starts at a very young age, when children begin to experience a variety of things and learn by following others within their family and within the educational setting. Children who attend a center full time will eat about half their daily food there, even more if they eat breakfast at the center. Therefore, it is imperative to ensure quality nutrition.

4.1 Healthy diet

More and more, the general public recognizes what nutrition specialists have advocated for some time: good nutrition preserves health. However, the North American way of life betrays serious discrepancies between discourse and reality. While 842 million of the planet's inhabitants suffer from hunger, a large number of other inhabitants suffer from overconsumption and poor nutrition. This causes many health problems—obesity, type II diabetes, cardiovascular disease, hypertension, hypoglycemia, digestive problems, high cholesterol, an excessively sedentary lifestyle, chronic fatigue, and weakening of the immune system.

In most cases, nutritional problems come from a lack of education about nutrition and a lack of interest. An apple is less expensive than a bag of chips. However, the latter often is the popular choice.

The nutritional value of ingested foods (vitamins, minerals, essential fatty acids, soluble fibers, proteins, and so forth) allow the metabolic functions to remain effective, an essential factor in staying healthy. Moreover, balanced nutrition increases attention span and aids learning in children (Hendrick 1988). It is essential to promoting overall health. Adults who are responsible for chil-

dren's nutrition should offer truly nutritious food. They should insist on freshness and variety, and they should provide items from all the food groups while at the same time reducing the servings of empty calories (sweetened fruit drinks, commercial cookies that contain a lot of sugar, artificially flavored crackers, and foods that contain chemical additives and preservatives).

Educators and parents may require that centers ensure only healthy meals and snacks are offered. They must clearly explain their point of view, and reiterate often the need to eliminate junk food such as chocolate bars, chips, sweets, and carbonated beverages.

> *Meals and snacks must include grains, fruits and vegetables, dairy products and alternatives, and meat (or meat substitutes). Portions should be tailored to the age group. Food service employees working at the center or the food caterer should follow the basic principles of healthy nutrition as well as governmental guidelines when they plan meals.*

It is feasible to offer healthy food at a reasonable price—food that is tasty, is healthy for body and mind, and does not take an overly long time to prepare. Numerous books on nutrition are available and may help educational centers to plan and prepare meals and snacks. Educators can also consult libraries and various associations and clinics to gather information on child nutrition.

4.2 Children's typical food preferences

As in other areas of development, the first years of life are vital for acquiring healthy food habits and knowledge. Educators need to clearly understand children's attitude toward food if they want to help children during this essential learning phase. Even though two- to six-year-old children show individual preferences, there are commonalities regarding their food choices. Box 4.1 lists some common characteristics:

BOX 4.1 **Typical childhood food preferences**

- Regular meal and snack times reassure children of all ages, not only the younger ones.

- Children prefer mild, salty, and sweet flavors. Usually they do not like exotic food, food that is bitter, or food that has a lot of seasoning, unless they were exposed to such foods at an early age.

- Most children enjoy eating bread, fruit, meat, and butter, but many dislike green vegetables. There are, however, ways to get them to try such vegetables.

- Since children's stomachs are small, they prefer to eat small quantities of food up to five or six times a day. It is important to offer three meals and two to three snacks a day.

- After the age of one, children like to recognize the food they are offered. It is best to offer them small separate portions rather than mixed foods. Cutting the food into small pieces is better than mashing or grinding it (do not hide it under a blob of ketchup or other sauce).

- Children prefer warm food to hot or cold food.

- Children like soft food in the beginning, and they start to enjoy crisp and crunchy textures later in life.

- Children enjoy easy-to-handle food such as soup in a cup, bread sticks and tofu dip, cut vegetables, cubes of cheese or tofu, pieces of fruit, whole wheat crackers, small pieces of meat, chicken nuggets, slices of whole wheat bread, oatmeal cookies, and so forth.

- Children enjoy looking at food. They like contrasting food colors, brightly colored place mats and dishes, and so forth.

In summary, children's food should be selected based on texture, color, shape, and nutritional value.

- From the age of one up to about five years, children's appetites fluctuate a lot, depending on their level of activity, physical shape, growing needs, and level of fatigue. They may also show extreme variations, such as devouring their food eagerly or refusing it within a short period of time. A child who is tired, emotionally unstable, or sick will generally have little or no appetite. The following factors inhibit a child's appetite: the peaks and valleys of growth spurts (characteristic of early childhood), infections (ear infections, gastroenteritis, colds, or bronchitis), immunizations, medications (antibiotics or acetaminophen [Tylenol]), and bronchodilators (inhalation aerosols such as Ventolin).

4.3 **Managing the task of meals and snacks**

Although good nutrition is essential, it is not enough. Also important is the type of setting where meals are taken. A quiet setting facilitates digestion and motivates children to eat. Indeed, meals at the center must be pleasant and peaceful periods for adults as well as for children. "Let us not forget that eating constitutes one of the wonderful pleasures of life" (Petit 1994, 47). Ensure that mealtimes are pleasant for the entire group. Box 4.2 includes suggestions that will help you achieve this.

BOX 4.2 **Managing meal and snack times**

- It is better to schedule lunch for children younger than age four early, around 11:30 AM, after outdoor play. Preschoolers can have lunch a bit later, around noon, before a nap that starts around 1:15 PM. Ultimately, each center should plan mealtimes around the children's needs.

- Plan thirty to forty minutes for lunch, thirty minutes for breakfast, and fifteen to twenty minutes for each snack. Allow enough time to avoid rushing children, but not so much that idleness results. A clock in the room makes it easier to manage time.

- Ideally, there should be a fifteen-minute buffer on the established schedule to start and end meals and snack without pressuring children because of a lack of time. Beware of the "infernal rhythm of life" imposed too often on children and adults alike. Centers should seriously analyze interventions that occur during meal and snack times to detect if their way of doing things meets the children's real needs.

- Warn children in advance that snack or mealtime is approaching. "After the ball game, it will be time for a snack." Preschool children learn fast how activities follow each other and may even sit down at the table without prompting.

- Adults and children must wash their hands with liquid soap from a dispenser and warm running water before touching and eating food. Moreover, educators must wash their hands between the preparation of different foods; for instance, when they prepare orange pieces after having cut cheese cubes. Do not wear bracelets or rings (food scraps and germs may get on or into them). Educators who have a skin injury on their hands must wear protective gloves.

- Young children should wear an apron or a bib to minimize the soiling of clothes—very important when spaghetti is on the menu!

- Sanitize the tables where children are eating before they sit down. Do not use spray sanitizer.

- As much as possible, limit waiting time before, during, and after meals and snacks. This will reduce unwanted behavior on the part of children. Take into account their level of development when asking them to be patient.

- Reduce as much as possible the time between food preparation, service, and ingestion to avoid the proliferation of bacteria. Foods that are easily contaminated should not stay in the temperature danger zone (between 40°F and 140°F or 4°C and 60°C) for more than two hours.

People assigned to food preparation must observe strict cooking and storage guidelines for food and ensure food safety and hygiene at all times. They must also take into account food allergies and intolerances, choking dangers, and religious and cultural restrictions.

- Put only a small amount of food on each child's plate. You can always give them seconds later. From age one on, it is best to start by offering one tablespoon of each food per year of age. For instance, two tablespoons of chicken, two tablespoons of rice, and two tablespoons of cut string beans for a two-year-old (Lambert-Lagacé 2000). For milk and juice, it is better to fill glasses half full or even one quarter full rather than forcing children to drink a full glass. Even for children with a normal appetite, eating a whole apple as a snack may be too much: give less, and give seconds when requested. When hungry themselves, educators have a tendency to serve too big a portion. Likewise, when parents prepare lunches, they also have a tendency to pack too much.

In the end, it is the responsibility of adults to offer a variety of quality food, and it is up to the children to determine how much they will eat (Lambert-Lagacé 2000).

- Have a clear agreement with parents whose children eat breakfast at the center. Who provides breakfast? Is there an extra cost? When is breakfast served? What is going to be on the menu?

- It is essential to get children used to drinking water during the day: during snacks, when coming back in from outside, on hot days, when performing high-energy activities, and so forth. Do not wait until children ask for a drink before offering water, since thirst is a sign that dehydration has already set in (Petit 1994, 108).

- Do not make children compete to finish their meal first. After suggesting that children taste all the types of food on their plate, it would be unfair to scold them for taking the time to do so! If a child is dawdling, just take away the plate or ask her to put away her lunch box while reminding her that she can eat more next time if she wants.

- To reduce traffic during meals, ask children to raise a hand when they need help.

- At the end of meals or snacks, ask children to wash their faces and hands with a wet cloth handed to them or, ideally, with running water and soap. This will remove food

scraps where bacteria thrive. Obviously, ban the use of a single cloth for all children, as well as the use of a single basin of water for all.

- Sweep the floor and the chairs, and wipe tables and chairs if needed, to avoid contamination by scraps of food. A child might pick up a crumb, put it in his mouth, and get sick.

- After meals and snacks, empty the garbage can filled with food scraps and sanitize its cover.

BOX 4.3 **Encouraging preschoolers' participation during meals and snacks**

- Ask children to distribute and pick up plastic glasses.

- For preschoolers, place food platters in the middle of the table or on an adjacent table to teach them to help themselves, while following the rule that they only put on their plate what they are going to eat.

- Ask children to clean up their places after eating, picking up whatever is left lying around and wiping the table and chair.

- Ask three- to five-year-olds to throw their garbage in the garbage can after the meal. This will teach them early on to care for their environment.

- Ask them to quietly push in their chairs when they leave the table.

- Ask them to sweep the floor around the table.

There are other ways to encourage positive behavior. Perhaps good behavior could be rewarded by giving children a necklace or a badge to wear. (Children must know in advance what type of behavior will be rewarded.) Or, each child could be challenged to clean up her place after meals during the early part of the week, to earn a privilege during the latter part of the week.

Privileges for the amount of food eaten or the time taken to eat should never be used. "If you eat everything on your plate," "The first one who finishes eating," or silence competitions are very negative. Values fostered by a good educational system should stimulate children, not humiliate, reprimand, or underestimate them. Besides, such strategies are ineffective since they are used to the exclusion of other strategies and since the same children are always rewarded.

In difficult situations (for example, a group of ten very excited four- and five-year-olds), have an extra helper available.

4.4 Physical and material organization

Room arrangement has an obvious influence on mealtimes. Educators must make sound choices regarding where and how meals and snacks take place.

The first principle is safety. During meals and snacks, you must enforce special guidelines and be particularly aware of children. Children are safer when they remain seated throughout the meal. This allows them to chew and swallow their food properly. Children should never lie down, run, cry, laugh, or sing when they eat. Moreover, they should never be left alone. If a problem arises, you must react immediately. Children should not feed one another, regardless of age. Exchanging or sharing food, whether from a plate or a lunch box, should be totally forbidden in order to ensure, among other things, that severely allergic children are protected.

> *Never take safety for granted during meals and snacks.*

The table arrangement should allow children to interact. A round table ensures that children see each other well and facilitates supervision. Sometimes children need to be seated apart from each other at different tables, but the arrangement must still allow for good overall supervision.

It is best that children not sit on the floor too long while eating. They get tired quickly without back support.

> *Long folding tables are easy to store. However, they discourage interpersonal communication. For pedagogic purposes, small round tables are best. These tables foster exchanges among individuals. They can be grouped in islands. Folding circular tables, seating eight to ten, with seats and backrests, are widely available.*

Since meals and snacks are great opportunities for social development, it is a good idea to modify the child groupings to encourage new interpersonal contacts. For example, you may allow children to eat their snacks at small tables seating two or three to encourage them to establish closer contacts with different group members.

You may want to rotate seating arrangements if conversations are otherwise difficult to encourage. Why not identify chairs with each child's first name or a personal symbol to help children find their place quickly and to surreptitiously solve conflicts among table neighbors? And remember, sitting next to the educator for a snack or a meal is a privilege young children usually enjoy.

Since we know that a high number of children in the same room greatly increases noise level, tension, and frequency of guidance interventions, it is important to limit as much as possible the number of children who need to eat at the same time in the same room. Sometimes it is better to have children eat in their usual homeroom or in another small room rather than gathering all the children in a noisy and impersonal dining room.

> *Who can endure for long a situation in which fifty, sixty, and even more children are squeezed next to each other, on benches without backrests, in a room with an intolerable noise level?*

On top of that, the children need to swallow their meal in a hurry to vacate the room for the next group. This situation puts too many demands on educators, and children have difficulty asking them for help. In such a stressful environment, children are subjected to an avalanche of guidance interventions that sometimes turn into threats and screams. How does such a crowded situation prepare children for their afternoon learning?

Although this description seems exaggerated, it reflects the reality at a number of centers. It is important to find solutions that benefit staff and children alike. There are several factors to consider when choosing a dining location.

A separate dining room has its advantages, including increased stability, nearby bathrooms, a change of environment for the children, and the separation from play material that may be distracting. However, a separate dining room does not provide as much intimacy as the regular room.

How is the noise level going to be controlled during meals to foster relaxation and personal exchange among the participants and to facilitate digestion? Consider the choice of music (loudness, pace, duration), noise from kitchen appliances and from dishes being handled, noise from the educator's guidance interventions, and so forth. Some centers use television or videos during snacks and meals to limit children talking among themselves. In this case, the rule is usually that everyone eats silently, and that the television or video plays only if the noise is kept low. Is this ideal for children who already spend twenty-five hours a week in front of a screen (television, videos, games), and when a third of a child's waking life is spent watching images that often trivialize violence, sex, and racism? This is a blatant example of contradiction between the values advocated by some educational settings and their practices. Despite considerable progress in recent years, pedagogical consistency in early childhood education is not yet a reality.

Can children be offered adequate space in which to take their meals and snacks without causing them to feel squeezed? Can the space be equipped with comfortable furniture, such as sturdy chairs with straight backs, adapted to their

size so that their feet touch the ground? Furniture designed for the space will also minimize spills and wastes. Can the educator be provided with a chair adapted to her needs and her size so she can sit during meals?

Relaxing during meals and snacks is not always easy. A table at chin height, low chairs that force children to sit on their knees, unsafe booster seats that contribute to falls, a rough table surface, a long sitting period, a noisy environment—none of these are conducive to the comfort and relaxation of children or educators during meals and snacks. Remember that meals and snacks will take place more than six hundred times a year!

Food should be served on easy-to-handle dishes that are shatterproof, solid, and have a large rim (Petit 1994, 49). Younger children should wear a bib. A plastic cloth under the table may be useful as a way of collecting food scraps, thus easing cleanup. Of course, an easy-to-wash floor is the best option, especially for home child care. Paper towels and cleaning cloths should be easily available. Preschool children should be encouraged to clean up their own spills and messes.

Not all children may want to have a snack in the afternoon. In this case, they should have access to a play space and to play materials. It is detrimental to these children to have to remain seated at the table and get bored while the other children eat, unless they want to be there, of course.

Snacks and meals can be enlivened by a change of setting, such as having a picnic outside under a tree, or, in the middle of winter, using a spring theme to decorate the eating space.

4.5 Creating a positive mealtime atmosphere

Your responsibility as an educator is to manage tasks and time, space, and equipment to ensure peaceful and relaxed meal and snack times. Moreover, your verbal and nonverbal communication has a great influence on the whole environment at mealtime. Indeed, it is hard to have a quiet meal if an educator is fussing constantly while children are eating. Rather than keeping busy, sit with the children and participate in the meal. Less moving around and more positive interpersonal contact will result in a calmer meal. If you stay at the table, it may be necessary to have a side table, a service cart, or a tray to facilitate service. Plan ahead for all necessary materials and equipment to be on hand so that tasks can easily be done at the table.

It is the educator's job to create a positive and friendly atmosphere during meals and snacks.

Smiling, looking at children, and being affectionate are concrete ways to create a friendly atmosphere. Children like it when their educators show humor, speak in a make-believe voice, take the role of a make-believe character, introduce a theme such as eating in a chic restaurant, and, in general, adopt behavior that makes mealtimes positive and relaxing. Sharing a meal can be a relaxing time with a bit of organization and a positive attitude.

Requiring absolute silence at the table is unnecessary, except in unusual situations, and for a limited time only. There are plenty of other means by which to induce calm during meals: setting a good example by whispering, congratulating children for their good behavior, asking children to rest their heads on the table for two minutes, using a puppet to give directions in a funny way, introducing interesting conversation topics, or suggesting a theme such as "name a funny snack." Remember to take a few slow and deep breaths to relax when children get too excited.

Preschool children often enjoy talking during meals and snacks. Encourage the quieter ones to speak by asking them questions or by making a few simple and personal remarks. At no time, however, should a child be forced to speak. Children enjoy informal exchanges when they can talk about what interests them. It could be about an approaching birthday, a recent trip to the movie theater, a family visit to a grandparent, a domestic animal, a new activity, a future event, and so forth. The list is endless.

Special occasions provide a good opportunity to modify the setting. Ideas for decorating the table are endless: laminated place mats (possibly made by the children), special tablecloths, a centerpiece with children's contributions, a small bouquet of flowers gathered during a walk (watch out for allergies), and so forth. Other changes include dimming the lights, playing soft music for a few minutes, or organizing picnics outside or in another part of the center. Such changes are very effective in breaking up the monotony of routines, and children of three years and older truly enjoy them.

4.6 Mealtimes with two-year-olds

Since infant growth slows down after one year, it is normal to see a significant decline in a child's appetite until he reaches five. It is best to respond to children's needs by adjusting portions.

Personal relationships with food are established early on, so it is important for adults to make wise selections for children in relation to food and nutrition. The significant adults, educators, parents, food service workers, managers, and board members should collaborate and agree on the main features of a center's nutrition program.

Decisions about nutrition greatly influence children's development, ability to concentrate, and their motivation. Parents sometimes relax their vigilance about their child's nutrition when the child reaches one year of age, even if they had been very attentive to the child during the first months of life. Therefore, educational centers must double their efforts to offer a healthy menu.

Children's emerging creativity from eighteen months to two years of age leads them to experiment with food. They need to be told clearly what is expected from them and to be gently redirected if they become distracted. "After your snack, you will be able to play with playdough, but now you need to eat your applesauce with your spoon."

It is not easy for two-year-olds to sit for thirty to forty minutes, especially if they are still using a high chair at home. This age group needs to be patiently and gently reminded of expectations if they are to learn new behavior. It is essential to limit the time they spend sitting, without, on the other hand, hurrying them. The golden rule is perseverance. Most children will meet their educator's expectations eventually.

Although some two-year-olds do not like to get dirty, it is reasonable to expect them to be messy while eating. They often ask for a napkin during meals so they can wipe their mouths and hands. They may wear aprons or bibs, and a plastic cloth can be spread under the table to facilitate cleanup after meals.

Around age two, young children also start to have specific likes and dislikes as far as food is concerned. They clearly express these, refusing to eat some foods they previously enjoyed and asking for other foods over and over again. Children this age are also developing the need to affirm themselves.

Since repetition, precision, and stability are distinctive features of this age group, it is best to maintain the same order in presenting foods, as well as the same habits, rituals, spatial organization, furniture, and so forth (Betsalel-Presser 1984).

Two-year-olds will frequently refuse to accept any changes in routine or in the environment. Therefore, it might be best to introduce new elements between the ages of one and two, when children are more open to change. Some examples: introduce the idea of sitting at the table instead of in the high chair, end the use of bottles or a special cup, replacing pureed food with conventional food, or introduce new flavors. Individual needs and situations must be considered; however, all food groups should be introduced before the age of two. Pureed food should be totally eliminated by age two-and-a-half, by which time children should have acquired all their baby teeth.

Educators caring for eighteen- to thirty-month-olds will find that the period preceding lunch is difficult. Some children will need a diaper change, while others have to be sat on the potty. Some will be tired from the morning activities, and others will have difficulty tolerating hunger. All this generates tension among peers and taxes the educator, who is also tired and hungry. Careful planning of the time surrounding lunch, while remaining flexible, will get the group through lunch with a minimum of stress.

4.7 Lack of appetite, refusal to eat, and other challenges

Educators are quick to notice when children are temperamental or refuse to eat. How should educators respond to this behavior? Is it better to go easy or to insist on compliance? To reason with a child or to fight with him? To suggest a compromise or to preach? To be confrontational or to divert the child's attention?

Several books give very good advice on how to intervene in an efficient way when children are not interested in eating. Many authors suggest observing children in an objective way to check that they have a good level of physical energy. Can children run, laugh, move with ease, and participate in activities? If so, there is no reason to be overly worried if they do not eat much during the day. However, it is best to continue to monitor the situation and to follow up with parents.

Some eating difficulties may grow out of anxiety-generating situations within the family or the center, such as a divorce, a staff change, or unemployment. However, in cases where children seem overly tired, refuse to participate in physical activities, have difficulty concentrating, have mood or sleep problems, seem underweight, or look sick without any specific symptoms (fever, cold, gastroenteritis), and when realistic solutions do not work, it is urgent to encourage parents to consult a health specialist. In other cases, it is best to play down the child's lack of appetite. As Louise Lambert-Lagacé (2000) reminds us, it is best to adopt an understanding and loving attitude when children show a lack of motivation toward food.

A. EATING PATTERNS AND CHILDREN'S TEMPERAMENTS

Children's individual personalities often affect their eating patterns. Some babies are enthusiastic eaters (Essa 1990); from their first feedings, they show a strong interest in food. Others worry their parents because of persistent colic or repeated regurgitation. To complicate matters, some children have food intolerance or feeding difficulties. Each child is unique in her attitude toward food.

> *Children's individual attitudes toward food and nutrition are marks of their uniqueness. Educators need to understand this and treat it with good judgment. They also need to cooperate with parents.*

Children who are labeled "difficult" have a tendency to become difficult (Essa 1990). They will sense if adults worry about their eating habits, even if those worries are expressed with great subtlety. It is a fact that such children are treated differently from others. Adults beg them to eat their meal, to taste some food, to finish their glass of milk, and so forth. With a bit of discernment, these children can easily counter the strategies used by parents and educators to ensure they eat well.

B. EATING PATTERNS AT DIFFERENT AGES

A child's age may explain some of his whims regarding food. Younger children only need small portions of food to meet their physiological needs. It is common to see children between ages one and six use refusal of (or preference for) food to establish their autonomy. This is a normal stage of socio-affective development, and such behavior will increase if the child sees adults worry or get angry about such refusals.

> *The best strategy to use if healthy children refuse to eat is to accept this fact without fuss.*

C. OBSERVING CHILDREN'S EATING PATTERNS

We may think, "This child never eats anything." In reality, things may be different. It is easier to generalize a worrisome situation than to look for facts and analyze them to find a solution. Is it really true that this child never eats anything? A systematic and professional observation will distinguish

facts from perceptions. Here are some questions that must be answered to identify the problem:

BOX 4.4 **Questions to ask when children refuse to eat**

How to identify a child who has eating problems.

Does the child:

- Stare at her plate or say she does not like the food?
- Refuse to eat green vegetables?
- Play with food?
- Have difficulty swallowing, or chew for a long time?
- Seem discouraged when there are too many things on his plate?

What foods are refused? What foods are preferred?

- Yogurt?
- Red meat?
- Citrus fruit?
- Other?

What behavior does the child display?

- No apparent reaction, no words?
- Complaints?
- Sadness?
- Loud crying?
- Keeping food in the mouth for a long time?
- Being aggressive or stubborn?
- Playing with food?
- Gagging? Stomachaches?
- Other?

Is it a recent problem? When did it start?

How often does this behavior appear within one week, and when does it occur?

- Twice during lunch, three times during snacks?
- Especially at the beginning of the meal?
- Other times or frequencies?

What happens when the child behaves like this?

- Does he eat selectively?

- Does she talk a lot during meals and snacks?
- Does an educator end up giving him two or three spoonfuls?
- Do other children ask her to eat?
- Is the atmosphere relaxed or tense?
- Other?

Once these observations have been objectively collected, an in-depth analysis will yield a more useful picture of the situation. Then you can share these observations with the other staff members at the center and devise an action plan. The input as well as the encouragement of all colleagues is beneficial to an efficient program. It is also necessary to inform the parents of the problem as it was identified, and the actions taken, since it will affect family life one way or another.

D. INDIVIDUAL EATING HABITS

Children and adults have individual eating habits. Consider those individual habits as well as family traditions regarding meals. Here are a few questions about individual habits: Does the child eat well? When does she have breakfast at home? Does he eat pears? What happens at mealtime? The answers will help you understand the child's behavior with regard to food.

Family food habits vary widely. They may include the consumption of fast food or spicy food. There may be no vegetables in the family diet. Mealtimes may vary. There may be various types of ethnic food. Food served at the center and general mealtime organization may not appeal to a child if these are very different from what occurs within his family. Despite such situations, it is best to offer children healthy food in a structured environment, while avoiding "pressure, constraints, blackmail and excessive attention given to children when they refuse foods" (Petit 1994).

> There is no place in an educational setting for statements such as "Eat or your daddy will not come to pick you up," "Eat your meat or you will not be able to go to kindergarten," "You need to finish your broccoli, or you will not get dessert," or "Who can finish their plate first?" Such interventions have no educational value and should be banned. Food should never be used as a reward or as a punishment.

Games such as "a spoonful for mommy," imitating a plane to encourage a child to open her mouth, or sitting close by to constantly encourage a particular child to eat should be used sparingly. In the long run, such practices end up being detrimental to a healthy attitude toward food. No matter what individual behaviors children show, they need to develop a positive attitude toward food, eating, and meals. They need to focus on the various sensations around eating (feeling hungry and full, likes and dislikes), and they need to establish the link between food and caring for oneself. Adults who use blackmail or manipulation will not help children develop healthy attitudes toward food.

> It is important to play down situations in which children refuse food or show little enthusiasm for it. Instead, work with parents to find solutions that foster healthy child development.

E. USEFUL MEAL AND SNACK STRATEGIES

It can't be stressed enough: Taking meals and snacks in a pleasant environment contributes to the pleasure of eating and tasting food and distracts children from thinking about a specific food they might dislike.

At times, it might be beneficial to firmly and calmly encourage some children to eat two mouthfuls (for two-year-olds), three mouthfuls (for three-year-olds), and so on. At the end of the meal, it is better to take the food away without commentary or disapproval. You may say to the child, "You will eat more next time!" The child might feel hungry until the next meal, a natural consequence of food refusal. Children know their appetite better than anyone else (Lambert-Lagacé 2000). Your role as an educator is to reward good eating behavior with a smile and a positive look, and to ignore more problematic behavior.

Joanne Hendrick (1988) suggests a little trick to encourage a child to eat if he does not like what is on his plate: "I think you will like this taste when you grow up!" For example, we can tell children that the new type of bread offered at snack time is an adult food that they can taste when they are ready to, or we can say that the green pepper on their plates would like to be digested, but to do that it must first go into their stomachs. "The pepper loves you to eat it, because it is doing its job." Some children like a bit of fantasy. A sound strategy to widen children's food preferences is to invite them to taste a particular food without forcing them to do so. When children dislike a particular food, it is good to keep offering it to them, because tastes and attitudes change over time.

On the other hand, it is not helpful to add more than one new food at a time, and when you do add a new food, you need to provide an alternate choice of familiar food and hold realistic expectations. Very young children prefer familiar foods, but as they grow up, they will try new foods. Foods such as mushrooms, olives, strong cheeses, or mussels with an exotic sauce are usually not children's preferred food! Moreover, it is useful to prepare children for a new food by taking the time to speak about it the day or the morning before. Chickpeas will be better accepted if children have the opportunity to look at and manipulate them beforehand, and if an educator explains where and how they grow, with the help of illustrations. When food is introduced, pedagogical techniques adapted to the level of the children's development have a positive impact on their receptions. The last part of this chapter presents learning activities to introduce children to new food.

When food is presented and displayed in an interesting way, children may be motivated to taste it. For example, tomato slices can be presented as a truck wheel, alfalfa sprouts as a little person's hair, apples can be cut out like stars, cheese pieces can be cut out with cookie cutters, and so forth.

Reduced portions are better for children than overflowing plates. Separate foods are more attractive than mixed ones.

Placing a child who eats well next to a lackluster eater is helpful in encouraging the lackluster eater to eat.

The example set by educators is also important. In the area of nutrition, your influence on the group should not be underestimated. Your verbal and nonverbal attitudes—interest in food or rejection of it, concealed disgust, or indifference toward new food and new flavors—are apparent to children.

When preschoolers can help themselves, it is easier for them to accept and to eat what is on their plates. It is wise to limit self-service to one part of the meal only, such as the main dish. For the initiative to be successful, you have to set clear and precise rules:

- Take a little of everything.
- Only take what you are able to eat.
- You will be able to come back for seconds if you are still hungry.

This approach is inappropriate with children younger than thirty months, and it requires patience if you want it to be successful. At the beginning, it is normal for children to put too much food onto their plates, even with clear guidelines. They are also clumsy and may spill food. Remember, they are learning, and the experience is worthwhile despite temporary inconveniences.

Children are more motivated to eat food they have helped to prepare. Plan simple culinary experiences with children, and then eat the prepared food for a meal or a snack. Preparing fruit skewers for snack, cutting up cubes of cheese for pasta, or slicing mushrooms for spaghetti sauce can all be done with children.

If you are worried about a child's eating behavior, you may use a reinforcement chart every time the child tastes foods offered at meals and snacks. Before adopting this method, the child and her parents both need to be informed. Moreover, this approach should remain confidential by posting the chart in a private place instead of where everyone can see it. To increase success, first offer foods the child likes, and have him choose the sticker to place on the chart. This approach has a better success rate if it is backed up by parallel strategies and verbal reinforcement. "You have tasted some meat, some rice, and a green bean. Good . . ." As the bad habits diminish, you can gradually dispense with the chart as well as the systematic verbal reinforcement.

F. EMOTIONS AND EATING HABITS

It is essential to include an analysis of the child's family situation or of the stress caused by changes at the center in order to explain new eating patterns. Emotions greatly alter appetite. Periods of integration or major stress are not the time to modify eating behaviors imported from home or from another center, such as drinking from a bottle past the normal age or eating bread and pasta exclusively. It will be easier to modify the eating behavior later, when things are calmer.

G. FOOD PREFERENCES

Children, like adults, have preferences. For example, foods such as brussels sprouts and beef liver are commonly unpopular. Food also needs to be prepared in an appetizing way. Some ideas are cream of broccoli, cauliflower au gratin, cubes of liver in a tasty sauce, shepherd's pie with lentils, and so forth. However, some children (and some adults) will always refuse to eat certain foods: turnips, fish, tomatoes, onions. Indeed, the aversion to certain foods is very real.

H. FLUCTUATING APPETITES

Finally, remember that some negative eating behaviors are temporary. Up to the age of five, children develop at a rapid pace. There are normal peaks and slacks in that development that may be very sudden. Eating behavior may fluctuate greatly and throw educators off. Nevertheless, it is important to offer children "unpopular" food regularly, without forcing them to eat it. Some children need to come to grips with a new food by looking at it on their plate a few times before deciding to taste it.

4.8 Eating habits and special diets

To aid in the social integration of children who belong to a particular culture, it is important to include on the menu items from various cultures. The whole group will benefit. Pureed sweet potatoes, mangos, different varieties of lettuce, pita bread, couscous, bagels, red kidney beans, and bulgur wheat will add variety and new colors, textures, and tastes that will arouse curiosity.

Food restrictions, whether cultural, religious, or family preference (no pork, no refined sugars, and so forth), need to be taken seriously. It is essential to have a clear agreement with parents to avoid any misunderstanding (Betsalel-Presser 1984).

Children are influenced by their family, especially their parents. Parents who don't eat breakfast themselves may not see the importance of providing breakfast for their children. If this is the case, the child may refuse to eat breakfast because of the parent's modeling (Pimento and Kernested 2004).

4.9 Overeating

"This child has an endless appetite." "His eyes are bigger than his stomach." These are comments commonly made about children who are fond of food. These children are attracted to food well beyond their real needs—they are excited around food. They may ask when it is time to eat. They might be afraid they won't receive something of every food being served. They swallow rapidly everything in front of them, and then ask for seconds. They grab food obsessively. At times, there is an uncontrolled urge to eat, a compulsive need to swallow large quantities of food.

With the help of parents and educators, these children can learn to have a healthier attitude toward food. While sharing meals and snacks with these children, educators can help them lessen their dependence on food. "We have to teach such children to listen to body signals related to eating, to make them aware of their real feelings of hunger and of satiation" (Petit 1997, 57).

The ability to differentiate between a desire for food and a real need to eat is learned at a very young age. Verbal interventions may help children become aware of their own body sensations. Here are a few examples: "You like this food so much that it is difficult for you to stop eating it!" "Do you feel hunger in your body?" "What does your tummy tell you?" "Your tummy is hungry? Your tummy is full? Your tummy wants more food?" "Do you have room for another apple?" It is good to often use phrases such as "Are you full?" "Are you satisfied?" "Have you eaten your fill?" Children need to be able to describe the feeling of being full, of their body having had enough food. The following educational interventions may be used with children who are fond of food.

- Teach moderation without guilt or comparisons between children. Offer compromises such as, "I will keep some for you for tomorrow, since I know you really like this food."
- Teach children how to make healthy food choices.
- Teach children to fully taste food and to enjoy eating slowly (not gulping food).
- Teach children to detect physiological signs of hunger and fullness.

Even young children have to develop a certain wisdom about food (Petit 1994). As educators, our responsibility is to encourage children to taste food to the fullest, to take the time to chew food, and to find pleasure in eating without gulping food or losing control, to decode the body sensations related to hunger and satiety (or of having eaten too much, such as nausea, bloated abdomen, pants too tight, and so forth). Take into account personal dislikes for certain foods, and don't forget that physical activities act as a regulator of hunger and need to be an inherent part of an overall health program.

Some children eat a lot without showing signs of obesity, while others may be overweight without eating too much. Nonetheless, it is now recognized that children who eat too much are likely to suffer from weight problems later in life. Weight problems in children are compounded by social problems (Essa 1990), since overweight children are perceived as different. They have a tendency to belittle themselves. They lack agility, will often have trouble following other children during physical activities, and are easily out of breath. This leads them to prefer quieter games. Obviously, their body image will be affected if they are the target of mockery by others and if they are constantly compared with other children.

Behavior related to food is not easy to modify since the food is associated with pleasure. If it is addressed in early childhood, when adults are still able to control a child's food intake, chances of rehabilitation are higher.

> *Moderate food intake and the choice of quality over quantity to meet the body's requirements are not so much questions of body weight and aesthetics, but of health.*

When a child displays a weight problem, a team approach led by parents, educators, and health and nutrition specialists has the best chance of success.

4.10 Table manners

"Showing children polite behaviors contributes to their development," says psychologist Jovette Boisvert (2000, 37). Learning to say *thank you, please, excuse me, good morning,* and so forth comes first and foremost through the example set by adults. Imitation is definitely a powerful learning tool for children as far as good manners are concerned. Children must also be clearly and calmly told what is expected of them: close the mouth while eating; do not drop food back on the plate from the mouth; say please and thank you. Some behavior should not be accepted: making bubbles with juice, throwing food, playing with mashed potatoes, spitting food, burping loudly. Again, a calm and firm reminder is in order in these situations. "Food should stay on your plate." "Chew your piece of apple well, and then swallow it." "Use your spoon to eat your potatoes." "You should say 'sorry' when you make noise with your mouth like that."

According to Boisvert (2000), example and guidance are not the only factors in learning polite behavior. You need to also take into account the child's age and temperament, intellectual limitations, difficulty in controlling emotions, regard for others, and so forth. Around three years of age, children become aware that being impolite can hurt, irritate, or make others uneasy. For instance, chewing with the mouth wide open may be disgusting to others and even prevent them from eating. In contrast, good table manners contribute to a positive eating environment. During meals, show children they have a role to play in their own well-being by praising good, polite behavior. This will encourage children to show the expected behavior. First and foremost, eating should be a pleasant activity that people enjoy sharing. Teaching polite behavior and respect for oneself and others contributes to children's social development.

Generally, children start to eat neatly around the age of three. That means they are able to keep their food on their plates and in their mouths, without much spilling on the floor, clothes, and table. Except for messy foods such as spaghetti, or food that can easily be spilled such as soup, children over age three are usually able to eat without too much mess.

Some children have problems eating neatly because of motor or hand-eye coordination problems. They have difficulty manipulating utensils and bringing the food to their mouths. This may be due to a developmental lag, but only an in-depth investigation by health professionals will be able to diagnose a problem for sure. Some children who have problems eating neatly may be trying to get extra attention from adults and from other children. There are also children who combine both types of difficulties: motor problems and a need for attention.

As mentioned earlier, environment greatly influences how children eat. They notice when educators stress cleanliness by serving food carefully, by creating a relaxed atmosphere, by setting the table with care. These actions encourage children to show their best behavior at the table. It is also essential to provide dishes and utensils that are easy to manipulate, light, and unbreakable. Dishes should be adapted to the food served. For example, gelatin is hard to eat from a flat plate. Children will be able to help themselves if the serving dishes are easy to handle. Finally, food cut into small pieces is easier to handle by children with motor difficulties. Sandwiches, for example, are easier to handle if they are cut into four pieces.

Educators should implement a systematic learning program for children who need to learn how to use a specific utensil. Learning to use a fork or spoon takes the same care as any other skill.

4.11 Allergies and food intolerance

Food allergies affect 1 to 2 percent of all adults and 5 to 8 percent of all children. An allergic reaction occurs when a particular food substance is perceived as an invader by the body, which then tries to defend itself by producing antibodies, provoking a strong, sometimes deadly, reaction. The most common foods that elicit allergies in young children are peanuts, nuts, fish, seafood, eggs, and milk products. Food intolerance is even more

common than food allergies. The body's reaction to food intolerance is less severe and therefore less dangerous than with food allergies. With food intolerance, the body does not have the proper enzymes to digest certain foods. These foods are commonly cow's milk and other dairy products, wheat, corn, soy, chocolate, citrus fruit, kiwifruit, strawberries, and food coloring.

Medications such as antibiotics may also cause allergic reactions or intolerances in children. Particular attention is required when administering a new medication to a child. It is a good idea for parents to start a new medication at home so they can check for side effects. Clinical symptoms of food/medication allergies or intolerances include gastrointestinal problems such as bloating, diarrhea, and abdominal cramps; skin problems such as a rash, eczema, red blotches, or scabs; and (most serious) breathing difficulties, typically an asthma attack or swelling of the mouth and throat. Other symptoms include headaches, irritability, and fatigue.

Symptoms of allergies or intolerance may appear immediately or up to twenty-four hours after the ingestion of the pathogenic food. Reactions tend to increase with each food ingestion. Therefore, a mild initial reaction may lead to a much more severe reaction if the same food is ingested later. Allergies may be more frequent in children younger than six, then disappear as the child grows older. They are common in children whose family members had or still have allergies. Unfortunately, allergies to peanuts and seafood can persist throughout life. Peanut and nut allergies are so prevalent, and their effects so severe, that a coroner has recommended avoiding all products containing even traces of nuts and peanuts (Petit). See Box 4.6 for steps to take in the case of an allergic reaction or food intolerance.

BOX 4.6 **Actions to take in case of allergies and food intolerance**

- Get accurate information from parents about the type of allergy the child has.
- Learn the common signs and symptoms.
- Learn which foods to eliminate (including those containing "hidden" allergens).

- Become familiar with substitutes of equivalent nutritional value.

- Establish a procedure to follow in case of a reaction.

- Clearly post information in the kitchen as well as in the classroom, where everybody, including substitutes or volunteers, will see it. The poster should include a picture of the child and the list of forbidden foods.

- Always study the list of ingredients on commercial products (chocolate cookies and even popsicles may contain traces of peanuts).

- As early as possible, make the child aware of his allergy and encourage him to inform others.

- Require or strongly request that persons with severe allergies wear a MedicAlert bracelet.

- Know at all times where the EpiPen kit (auto-injector) is kept, and learn how to use it.

- Always take the EpiPen along during outings (to parks, museums, and so forth).

4.12 Choking dangers

Children can choke easily, especially those younger than three. Every year, a significant number of children between ages two and five die of asphyxiation because their respiratory tract is blocked by food or by an object. Others undergo an operation to dislodge an object stuck in the esophagus, the larynx, or the bronchial tubes. Prevention is obviously the best way to eliminate such accidents. One preventive measure is to teach children how to chew.

Among foods that present a choking risk are cylindrical shaped foods such as hot dogs or sausages (whole or sliced—remember to slice them lengthwise); whole grapes (they must be cut in two if they are fairly big); hard foods such as raw vegetables (carrots, cauliflower, or broccoli—it is better to steam them for a few minutes before serving them); leafy vegetables (cut them small); all types

of nuts; popcorn; large cubes of meat; hard candy; chips; and raisins. Watch for bones (especially fish bones), fruit stones and pits, and apple cores.

Toothpicks used as decorations are also dangerous. It is best to remove them completely when preparing food for children.

Choking signs include a sudden refusal to swallow, increased saliva, chest pain, difficult or noisy breathing, and blue lips or face. When a child seems to be choking on something, first observe the child closely. If there is crying or breathing, do not take emergency action. Instead, encourage the child to cough by helping him to bend forward. Do not slap him on the back or move him rapidly since that could move the object down the respiratory tract. It is important to help the child stay calm and to rapidly notify emergency services, which are better equipped to deal with the situation.

If breathing has completely stopped and the child cannot speak or cry or only emits a high pitched sound, the Heimlich maneuver should be undertaken immediately. A description of this maneuver can be found in Box 4.7.

BOX 4.7 **Heimlich maneuver**

- Call emergency services. Ask any other adult present to make the call, and then supervise the rest of the group. Shout "help" or send an older child to find another adult if needed.

- If the child is conscious, kneel behind her and place your arms around her waist.

- Make a fist with one of your hands and place it just above the child's belly button, thumb on the abdomen. Grab your fist with your other hand and give fast thrusts upward (J movement).

- Continue thrusts until the object is expelled.

- Remember to apply less force for smaller children.

- Once the maneuver is successful, consult a health specialist to assess if there is any further injury.

- All educators must be trained to perform emergency measures when required.

Note: This is not a complete first-aid procedure. Please consult your first-aid manual for further details.

4.13 Nutrition education

Nutrition is a popular theme for children. Food fascinates young ones as well as older children because it is linked to pleasure. Why not give nutrition a much larger place in the yearly and daily program than what is usually planned? There are numerous opportunities to try various approaches to the topic of nutrition.

A. ENCOURAGING CHILDREN'S PARTICIPATION DURING MEALS

Children learn a lot by participating in the preparation of meals and snacks. "Children 2 to 12 always enjoy cooking activities" (Petit 1994, 63). To motivate children on a rainy day, or to present something new in the daily schedule, why not ask children to wash and place fruit in a serving dish, or cut out commercial bread dough, then bake it for a snack? Cooking activities develop motor abilities, autonomy, and self-respect. Box 4.8 lists ideas to encourage participation.

BOX 4.8 Ways children can contribute to meals and snacks

Food preparation:

- Help wash fruit.
- Help place fruit or vegetables on individual plates or on platters.
- Decorate a plate with small dried fruits.
- Peel fruit such as clementine oranges. (Make a dent in the peel to help children get started.)
- Pour juice into glasses with a small pitcher. A 16 oz (500 ml) plastic cup is easy to use.

Actions around meals and snacks:

- Wash hands before and after.
- Set the table with a nice tablecloth or individual place mats. Decorate the center of the table with wild flowers or a centerpiece made in class.
- Help with service (distribute glasses and utensils).
- Pass a food platter.
- Help themselves from a food counter (side table).
- Clear off the table.
- Clean up the table.
- Sweep the floor.
- Put chairs back in place.

B. FOOD AWARENESS

Children learn good life habits from live examples. Much more than sermons and speeches, good models help children to acquire good habits and attitudes. Educators have a responsibility to be sound models.

Consistency between what is said and what is done does not come easily, especially during special celebrations when children often receive contradictory messages. Often, very sweet desserts, soft drinks, chocolate, and chips appear on the menu during "special" occasions. This is confusing for children. A four-year-old may reason, "My educator teaches me, through all sorts of interesting activities, that cola is not good for my health. However, today, I am allowed to have some because it is a special occasion. I really do not understand why. And she drinks cola and seems to like it." Because of their educational mission in regard to children and their families, child care centers should make a constant effort to select healthy foods for special occasions, celebrations, and fundraising campaigns.

It is estimated that children consume three or four foods that have no nutritional value every day (Petit 1994, 224), either at home or in restaurants. Without advocating a total ban on these foods, educational centers have a responsibility to be consistent with the educational values they promote, and this has to be reflected at all times, including on "special days." For special occasions, preschool children can participate in planning a menu comprised mostly of nutritious foods but including a few treats.

C. INTRODUCING NUTRITION THROUGHOUT THE CURRICULUM

1. Food theme at circle time
In educational centers, mealtimes total about two hours a day (two half-hour snacks and a forty-five minute lunch). These are golden opportunities to discuss food with children, ask them questions, and observe them. Your curiosity about food in the presence of children opens the door to fascinating knowledge (Petit 1994, 218).

When talking about food and culinary matters, use precise and correct language. There are many books for children about nutrition and food. Local libraries and professional associations are a source of references on the subject. With children ages four and older, start pointing out information about food and food content: too much sugar, not enough vitamins, unhealthy excess fat, and so forth.

2. Food-themed activities
Cutting out various food pictures from supermarket flyers can be a basis for learning about food, depending on the children's interests and capacities. Sensory exploration and simple cooking activities can also be very interesting. See Box 4.9 for food-themed activities.

BOX 4.9 **Ideas for food-themed activities**

- Cut out food illustrations and group by category (milk products, vegetables and fruit, meat and meat substitutes, bread and cereals, and junk food). Post them to stimulate conversation or put them in a personal folder of healthy food.
- Make a mobile from food illustrations to hang on the ceiling.
- Make a deck of food cards for guessing games, sorted according to taste, color, shape, and so forth.
- Make food puzzles by pasting food images on cardboard.
- Make a snake-and-ladder game with the four food groups and junk food.
- Describe a food from an illustration or a real example: shape, size, smell, texture, origin, culture, transformation, nutritional value, and so forth.
- Compare characteristics of foods within a category, such as the various shapes of pasta, different types of bread (whole wheat, rye, oat, etc.), or various types of apples.
- Identify foods by their smell or their taste.
- Prepare easy and nutritious recipes: oatmeal cookies, gelatin, fruit salad, blueberry muffins, yogurt dips, fruit punch, fruit smoothies, and so forth.
- Do some gardening. Plant alfalfa, aromatic herbs, beans, or another easy-to-grow vegetable.

Note: Generally avoid art activities that use food since these teach children to waste food. Such activities include printing with food, making necklaces with pasta, making collages with pasta or legumes, and so forth.

During snacks and meals, there are plenty of opportunities to explore food using the five senses.

Ask children to describe the visual aspects of food: colors, various shades of colors, consistencies (cooked, raw, crunchy, solid, liquid, soft, pureed), textures (shiny, thick, smooth, clear), shapes and volumes (large, small, round, cube, square, stick, slice, circle, oval, thick, thin, long, short).

Phrases like "It looks good," "It makes me want to eat," and "Your plate looks pretty" help children focus on what is on the table.

Here are some other suggestions to help children focus on food:

- Use remarks children make about food to introduce new characteristics about food: the brown spots on banana peels, the texture of a clementine orange peel, the small seeds of a kiwifruit, fruit found inside yogurt.

- Serve fruit (oranges, apples) or vegetables (carrots, cauliflower) in a creative way: cut them into quarters, thin slices, triangles, or fine strips. Cut apples or pears horizontally into thin slices to show the star heart.

- Make food arrangements such as little people, crowns, faces, or houses, or make skewers. Use cookie cutters to cut sandwiches, cookies, frozen treats, or gelatin shapes.

- Smells provide endless exploration activities. Try to identify the smells coming out of the kitchen. Smell food before eating. Compare smells. Make comments and ask questions related to the sense of smell. "It smells good. What does it smell like?" "The slice of bread does not smell the same as the cheese cube." "Where does this smell come from?" "Do you smell onion coming from the kitchen?" "Mmm! It smells like orange! Who brought one for snack?"

- Questions about food taste can enhance children's awareness: "What is sweet, salty, sharp, bitter, acid?" "Too salty?" "Too sweet?" "Does it taste burnt?" "What seasoning do you taste in this food? Mint? Garlic? Thyme? Cinnamon?"

- Children can be encouraged to detect various temperatures. Experiencing hot, warm, and cold food will enhance their perception. Eating also involves tactile sensations inside the mouth. "Is it hard or soft?" "How does the frozen yogurt feel in your mouth?" Use terms that describe consistency and textures such as *tender, moist, lumpy, creamy, thick, rubbery, sharp, melting, soft, fibrous,* and *hard.*

- Even hearing has its place in the sensory exploration of food. For example, draw attention to the sound foods make when manipulated or when eaten. "Listen to the sounds made by your crackers when you bite them." It is possible to describe a great variety of sounds related to food: simmer, fry, bubble, boil, chew, sip, grind, crunch, flow, and so forth.

3. Materials for dramatic play

The pretend play area can be equipped with a kitchen complete with accessories: plastic food; empty (but secure) cans; plastic jars; real kitchen tools such as spaghetti tongs, wooden spoons, colanders, garlic crushers, ladles, and cake molds; and empty food boxes (cereals, rice, pasta, eggs, muffin mix). Children will greatly appreciate service trays, aprons, oven mitts, individual table mats, various plastic containers, and illustrated recipe books.

Arrange a realistic grocery store with a shelf, a shopping basket or cart, a cash register (toy or homemade), play money, pencils and paper with which to write shopping lists (or to pretend to), food fliers, labels to post prices, bags for groceries, and so forth. Children can play the role of cashier or shopper. This is a favorite during free-play activity.

4. Educational field trips

Various visits can be organized to promote food-related learning: a traditional bakery to taste bread hot from the oven, an orchard, a local farm, a fruit and vegetable store or market, a supermarket to identify healthy food, or a restaurant kitchen (outside of peak hours). Prepare these outings with care to ensure their success.

5. Other games

Play restaurant: It is not enough to tell children to play restaurant. Really set the stage for children to get interested in the game. Have food-related art projects at the table for "customers" to pass the time while they wait to be served. Waiters and waitresses can take orders and serve customers. Customers can pay the check with play money at the end. If you are motivated, you will motivate children, and everyone will enjoy the experience. Variations: go to an Italian restaurant (find Italian food items) or another regional or ethnic cuisine, or wear a costume.

Play customs officer: Educators check the lunch boxes to "detect" peanuts or other allergenic foods. (Five-year-olds.)

Eat with eyes closed, like a person who is blind: Children can concentrate on other sensory perceptions.

Prepare a picnic: Prepare a picnic in the room, and pretend it is a special environment: a beach, a field of golden wheat, the edge of a forest, another planet, a winter camping site, and so forth. A special ambiance can be created using various materials: drawings, posters, pictures, fabric, recordings, costumes, and so forth.

Songs and rhymes: Songs and rhymes can enhance the beginning of meal or snack time. For example, sing this song to the tune "I'm a Little Teapot":

> *I'm a little apple*
> *On the ground,*
> *Fresh and juicy,*
> *Sweet and round.*
> *If you take a big bite*
> *Out of me,*
> *You'll find me tasty*
> *As can be.*

5

Nap or Relaxation Time

CHAPTER CONTENTS

5.1 The need to rest and refresh the body and the mind

5.2 Children's sleep patterns

    A. Naptime for children who sleep

    B. Naptime for children who do not sleep

5.3 Requests from parents

5.4 Room arrangement

5.5 Materials and equipment

5.6 Preparation and implementation

5.7 Getting up from nap

5.8 Other factors that affect nap and rest time

5.9 Games to introduce rest time

Rest and sleep are basic needs for children. Anyone caring for young children recognizes the need for a nap or rest period in the middle of the day. Studies show a generalized drop in concentration during the day between 11:00 AM and 2:00 PM and at night between 2:00 AM and 5:00 AM. Generally, children show signs of fatigue after lunch. This is when children are most likely to be sleepy and have decreased motor and physical performances (Thirion and Challamel 1999). Signs include a drop in concentration, apathy, irritability, and restlessness.

5.1 The need to rest and refresh the body and the mind

Rest is a normal physiological need. At all ages, there are certain signs of sleepiness—slower reflexes, relaxation of the muscles, yawning, sighing, tingling eyes, red eyes, feeling chilly, reduced visual focus, low tolerance for noise, and loss of appetite. Behavior is also affected: loss of concentration, less motivation, irritability, and nervousness. Since children's days at the center are filled with all sorts of activities and constraints, it is normal for them to get tired. Follow a child through a whole day to assess the magnitude of constraints he must face: there are rules about group life, safety requests, guidance and participation rules, materials to put away, peers to adapt to, and group movements to follow. Also consider that children have to adapt to a way of functioning in the center that differs from the one at home. For instance, there are more noises and more adults (including extra hands at lunchtime and during the educator's

break, substitutes, and so forth). All of this makes it even more important to plan a nap for the children in the middle of the day. Children may sleep or not, but this rest time is an important way of minimizing the cumulative effects of fatigue and of refreshing children physically and mentally.

5.2 Children's sleep patterns

Children's sleep patterns vary according to age, temperament, biological rhythm, spent energy, health, and heredity. At an early age children show characteristics of being heavy or light sleepers and early or late risers.

Humans sleep in cycles of five distinct steps (see Figure 5.1). In children, each cycle lasts about ninety minutes, and the cycle is repeated during the night as many times as necessary to get the required rest and to achieve biological and psychological growth functions.

Sleep and rest are just as essential to childhood health as food and hygiene. They contribute to children's physiological and psychological balance, and in particular to the development of mental functions such as memory and attention. "Educators balance the needs of the group with those of the individual" (Pimento and Kernested 2004, 422). Depending on the specific stage of sleep, children's brains continue to assume essential functions, such as the production of growth hormone (somatotropin). This hormone fosters growth and participates in the repair of damaged tissue and cells. During sleep, the brain also records and organizes information acquired during the day and resolves tensions accumulated during the day.

FIGURE 5.1 **Stages of a sleep cycle (± ninety minutes)** (taken from Thirion and Challamel 1999)

I	II	III	IV	V	Intermediary stage
Drowsiness stage. Falling asleep.	Light sleep stage.	Slow-wave and deep sleep stage. (Secretion of growth hormone.)	Paradoxical sleep. (Dreams.) (REM.)	Light sleep stage.	Waking stage or start of another cycle. Light sleep resumes.

"Sleep, good sleep, is essential to the functioning of the brain" (Thirion and Challamel 1999, 13). In summary, sleep and rest are directly involved in the growth and general development of children.

"Has this child gotten enough sleep?" "Does he need to rest this afternoon?" These are questions educators and parents ask themselves often. In reality, the only true indicator of whether or not a child has had enough sleep is her general behavior during the day and when she wakes up. Is she alert, and does she feel well? (PROSOM 2006). The same can be said for relaxation. Has the child had enough relaxation to renew his energy and to be able to pay attention? If this is not the case, ask why, and find out how to solve the problem.

The sleep needs of children during the day vary according to age, the amount of night sleep received, the amount of physical energy spent during the morning, and their general state of health. Some children stop taking an afternoon nap around the age of four, while others continue to need a nap until about six years of age (Thirion and Challamel 1999). Generally, two- and three-year-old children need fourteen hours of sleep daily, spread between night and the beginning of the afternoon. Children ages four to six need about twelve hours of sleep daily, spread between a night and an afternoon nap or rest. Finally, ten-year-old children need about ten to eleven hours of sleep daily, and sleeping needs decrease to eight hours daily for adults. These are averages and not strict norms to be applied to all children.

A. NAPTIME FOR CHILDREN WHO SLEEP

When children sleep during afternoon nap, it is best to let them sleep at least for the duration of a ninety-minute sleep cycle (seventy minutes for two-year-olds). Ideally, children should be left to sleep as long as they want and to wake up according to their needs. Contrary to popular notions, a nap during the day does not diminish night sleep, especially if it takes place right after lunch and does not last longer than one cycle, or seventy to ninety minutes (PROSOM 2006). People who believe that children will fall asleep earlier at night or that they will sleep longer in the morning when afternoon naps are eliminated are wrong. The opposite is more likely to happen, since children who become used to resisting their need to sleep during the day will try to do the same at night.

B. NAPTIME FOR CHILDREN WHO DO NOT SLEEP

Even if children up to kindergarten age are expected to lie down for a nap, they can in no way be kept still too long on their cots. After a reasonable period of rest, nonsleepers should be allowed to play quietly under the supervision of an educator, preferably in another room. Up to the age of three-and-a-half to four years, most children will sleep one or two hours during afternoon nap. Older children will sleep less or not at all. However, they will learn to stay quiet for some thirty minutes, and this can contribute to their attention, listening, and observation skills (Larose 2000). "Preschoolers, especially the older ones, don't require a nap any longer but still need to slow down and rest" (Pimento and Kernested 2004, 422).

Children who do not fall asleep during the first half hour of naptime usually do not need to sleep. This is often the case with children four and older. They should not have to remain on their cots longer than that, especially if they look uncomfortable there. It is best to offer them other ways to rest. The rest period for nonsleepers needs to be properly planned. "Just lying on a cot does not necessarily lead to relaxation" (Lauzon 1990, 234). Some breathing and gentle gymnastic exercises adapted to children may lead to efficient relaxation. This chapter includes some ideas for games to make nap a positive and restful experience.

Many centers favor a nap period of thirty to forty-five minutes between 12:30 and 2:00 PM, during which nonsleepers lie quietly on their cots. A period of calm and solitary play follows—drawing, puzzles, books—in a separate area of the room or in another room if an educator is available to provide adequate supervision. Other centers schedule a nap for older children only three times a week, at the beginning, middle, and end of the week. This makes sense because children seem to be more tired on Mondays and Fridays. Some centers require rest only on those days.

Children cannot be ordered to sleep, nor can their brains be forced to sleep, but the right conditions can help: darkness, calm, a loving attitude, stability, and verbal directions given softly and firmly.

Directions such as, "Lie down. . . . Close your eyes and sleep. . . . Stop moving. . . ." do not help children to relax, nor does trying to hold children down on their cots or patting their backs rapidly.

> It is essential to have an understanding of sleep and rest to adequately plan for naptime, and to adopt attitudes that will lead children to a proper relaxation level.

Preschool children benefit from a relaxation period at the beginning of the afternoon, before they undertake formal learning activities. Their attention level increases when they benefit from relaxation and stretching exercises to eliminate some of the tensions gathered through the first part of the day.

5.3 Requests from parents

Exasperated parents who have difficulty putting their children to bed at night often ask educators to suppress or shorten the afternoon nap. In such a case, educators should discuss the problem with the parents to find solutions that respect the child's

vital need for rest. Parents can be offered a compromise that satisfies them while respecting the child's needs. Thirty minutes of rest on a cot, followed by restful activities, might be the solution. Some parents ask educators to make their child sleep during naptime because she went to bed late the night before or had a bad night. Unfortunately, children cannot catch up on their sleep that easily. Rather, it is the child's general condition during the day that will dictate the necessity of a nap or rest during the afternoon.

Would parents ask educators not to feed a child at lunch so that he would have more appetite at supper time? No; they know that eating is a need that must be satisfied when hunger is present. It is a simple question of health. Our task as educators is to make parents understand that sleeping is as vital as eating and that it must be accommodated.

Parents and staff must have a clear understanding of the duration of naptime for nonsleepers. If you judge that a particular child needs a traditional sleeping nap, you need to communicate diplomatically to the parents your reason for allowing their child to sleep. For example, "A nap increases a child's attention and acts as a mood regulator for the rest of the day, which could be much appreciated during family supper time. Naps also lower the frustrations of group life. Finally, naps prevent the overtaxing of the child's energy, which is often a cause of frustration at bedtime."

Box 5.1 provides suggestions for educators and parents on deciding how to handle naptime when there are bedtime or nighttime sleep problems.

BOX 5.1 Suggestions for working with parents on sleep issues

- Show empathy when parents have difficulty putting their child to bed at night. Parents' daily lives can be very demanding, as in this example of a typical day in the life of a single mother of two.

  It is 6:00 AM. Martine gets up. She takes a hurried shower, prepares breakfast, wakes up the children, and prepares lunch for herself and the older child. Then she makes the beds, gives the cat his food, and eats break-fast while encouraging the children to do the same. She picks up what is scattered around and tries not to forget anything before she leaves home. She takes the older child to his school, then takes the younger one to the center, where she has to leave her crying. She feels guilty about it but needs to rush to get to work in the morning traffic. She works under pressure for the greater part of the day. During her break, she makes a dental appointment for the children. At 4:45 PM, she leaves work. During the half-hour drive in afternoon traffic she thinks about supper and everything else that awaits her at home. She stops at the cleaners and at the supermarket and then picks up the children. She prepares supper while trying to listen to the children, and she tries to keep her cool when a fight erupts between them. Then there is supper and dishes to be washed. She helps the older one with homework, gives a bath to the younger one, and does a load of laundry. She prepares the children for bed, loses her patience when the younger one refuses to go, then feels guilty because her daughter cries. Finally, she opens the mail (unopened for three days) and listens to the messages on her voice mail. It is 8:30 PM, and the day is not yet over. Martine, out of breath, hopes to have a few minutes to herself before bedtime . . . if her three-year-old daughter stops asking her for hugs, cuddly toys, to go to the bathroom, or for a glass of water, as she has been doing for half an hour. Martine also hopes no unforeseen events occur, because she is at the limit of her tolerance. She thinks of the constant nightmares her oldest child has been having for two weeks. Now it is 9:30 PM, and Martine thinks about her day. She feels incompetent and out of breath. Things are not going as she would like. She remembers that she has to bring a change of clothes to the center for her daughter. Her older child wakes up in tears. He had yet another nightmare. She takes the time to reassure him. Then she remembers she has to fill in the meningitis immunization form

her son brought back from school. Finally, Martine goes to bed. She has difficulty falling asleep because she is so tired.

Obviously, this mother is constantly stressed by the thousand-and-one tasks required by her professional life and family life. Pointing a finger at her for not being able to make her child sleep at night would only increase her feeling of incompetence, and she might end up mistrusting the educator. On the other hand, if she feels that someone is listening to her and understands what she is going through, she might be more inclined to consider another point of view for the good of her child.

Another difficulty that arises at bedtime is that parents who do not see their children during the day feel guilty about it and hesitate to be firm with them in the evening. In this case, if parents feel understood, they will be more receptive to your advice and will cooperate more readily. You help parents greatly when you show a positive attitude.

- Reassure parents that their child's bedtime refusal is normal. Around age two or three, children become very curious about their environment. They are aware that life continues even as they sleep, so they do not want to miss anything. It is also at this age that nightmares start, and they can continue up to the age of eight. Young children tend to have an overactive imagination, so a fear of wolves, thieves, or ghosts interferes with going to bed and letting sleep take over. Happily, in most cases, these sleeping problems are transitory and minor. If necessary, parents should consult a health professional. Sleeping problems are referenced by parents in a third of pediatric consultations. Real sleeping problems, however, are apparent in one out of five visits to the pediatrician (Thirion and Challamel 1999, 10).

- Compromise with parents who ask you to wake their child during naptime. You can suggest that naptime be shortened if their child is not asleep after thirty or forty-five minutes, a common situation with four- and five-year-olds. Quiet, individual activities can replace traditional naptime: books, puzzles, drawing, and so forth. For preschoolers who do not sleep, time spent lying down doing nothing seems endless, leading them to hate naptime. Forcing children to lie still for more than thirty minutes is cruel. These children can be offered alternate activities tailored to their needs.

- Explain to parents that the scheduled rest time is meant not to relieve you of your duties but to meet the children's needs. Obviously, the reality should reflect this statement!

- Parents may not be aware of the physiological aspects of the sleep process. You may suggest books, Web sites, fliers, or associations that promote sleep education. Post articles on the bulletin board that emphasize the link between naptime and children's well-being. A better understanding of the subject will help lessen worries and a feeling of helplessness when sleep difficulties occur. By helping young children acquire healthy sleep habits, parents can prevent sleep problems later in life.

- Without trying to be an expert, suggest that parents modify the family routine during the evening to ensure the required atmosphere at bedtime. Make sure they know the signs of falling asleep: yawning, rubbing eyes, and so forth. Suggest a routine of calm activities and parent-child communication: Give the child some attention at the beginning of the evening. Switch off the television and video games thirty minutes before going to bed. Give the child a ten-minute warning, dim the lights, play soft music, perform the evening hygiene routine, read a soothing story that the child likes, speak with a soft voice, and get the child to put on pajamas by himself. Children experience going to bed as a separation from their parents. Parents

can help them by using security items: a doll, a favorite soft toy, a night light, a favorite blanket or bedsheet (that children often suck on), a door left half open, and so forth. Medications to induce sleep should be given only when prescribed by a physician. Some herbal teas, lukewarm or warmer, not too concentrated, and lightly sweetened with honey may help induce sleep. Chamomile, orange blossom, and linden herbal teas are among the most effective. Mint, on the other hand, has stimulating properties. Parents who are given enough information on sleep usually find the solution to their child's bedtime problems—falling asleep late or refusing to go to bed—by themselves.

BOX 5.2 **Suggestions for parents on bedtime rituals that you can customize as a handout, post on a parent bulletin board, or include in your newsletter**

Kendall, four years old. Ritual starts at 7:25 PM. Ends around 8:00 PM.

- Bath, supervised by Dad.
- Pajamas.
- Toothbrushing by Dad.
- Soothing story read by Mom on the child's bed.
- Hugs from Dad and Mom.
- Good-night kisses. "Sweet dreams, lovely boy!"

Simon, eight years old. Ritual starts at 8:00 PM. Ends around 8:30 PM.

- Shower taken alone (however, a bath might be more relaxing).
- Pajamas.
- Toothbrushing by himself.
- Soothing reading done alone in bed.
- Hugs from Mom.

- Small talk (they talk about something nice that happened that day).
- Kisses. "Sleep well, Simon. I love you."

Laura, thirty months old. Ritual starts at 7:00 PM. Ends around 7:30 PM.

- Bath and water play with Mom.
- Toothbrushing by Mom.
- Small massage with soothing music enjoyed by the child.
- Hugs and child's favorite song, sung by Mom.
- Placing Laura's favorite soft toy in her arms.
- Kisses. "Good night, my angel. Sweet dreams."

Note: It is unnecessary to implement a lengthy bedtime ritual. What is important is that the ritual ends in the bed where the child will spend the night, and that there is quality time spent with the child. The bedtime ritual will be efficient if there is consistency and regularity.

5.4 Room arrangement

Children who usually sleep well during naptime should be placed along the walls away from the center of the room so they will not be disturbed by other children getting up in the middle of naptime. Generally, children feel more secure if they are always assigned the same place. Determine the best location to induce calm for each child. A plan showing the placement of cots or mats should be posted in the room for all staff to see. Some four- and five-year-olds may ask to change places for naptime, so you may need to try out a new arrangement. However, the ultimate arrangement is best left to your judgment. There are no firm rules; you'll need to solve problems case by case.

5.5 Materials and equipment

The right attitude is not enough to enable children to have a good nap. They also need adequate equipment, specifically clean and comfortable cots or mats. In fact, it is essential to have optimal materials for naptime. Each child should have a soft mat or cot in good condition, easily movable, with a washable cover. Cots or mats must be identified with the name or symbol of the child using it. After nap, covers must be removed and mats or cots sanitized, then stored, preferably in a closet with individual compartments. Parents should provide a blanket or a sheet that covers the child well. Plan to have changes of bedding in case of emergency. Bedding needs to be washed once a week—usually by parents—or more often if it is dirty. It must be stored in an individual cubby, basket, or closed bag to avoid contact between children's bedding. In a kindergarten, where a mat or cot is not always available, a large towel, although not ideal, allows a child to lie down for about fifteen minutes.

A comfortable rocking chair will allow you to rock a child who may be having difficulty calming down.

5.6 Preparation and implementation

From the time they wake up in the morning until the beginning of naptime (around 1:00 PM), children have about six or seven hours filled with all sorts of activities. Before even planning for nap, it is important to analyze the schedule of morning activities to ensure there are relaxation periods. Box 5.3 offers some advice about this.

BOX 5.3 **Suggestions for planning relaxation activities**

- During the first part of the day, follow a fixed schedule to provide children with a sense of security. Ensure a positive emotional atmosphere within the group and for each child. Use humor, fun, and tenderness.

- During the morning, plan physical games that children are interested in, as well as an outside play time. Children need to expend their energy in a secure environment adapted to their stage of development.

- Provide rest periods every sixty to ninety minutes. These could be short activities lasting from two to ten minutes to allow children to rest their brains after a period of intense concentration. Children could nestle their heads in their arms at the table or practice a few breathing and stretching exercises. These short rest periods renew body and mind, allowing children to wind down gradually and preventing the accumulation of fatigue that constitutes a major obstacle to the afternoon nap.

- Plan a transition period between lunch and naptime with calm games or play that the children enjoy. After children have spent forty-five minutes sitting down for lunch, they need to stretch their legs a bit before lying down. Personal hygiene activities allow children to move: going to the bathroom, brushing teeth, washing hands, taking off shoes. However, it is best to keep these activities short so that the children benefit from the optimal conditions for rest. (Their

need for food and drink has been satisfied, and they normally feel tired at this time.)

- Implement a predictable and stable nap routine. This will contribute to an atmosphere of security that is necessary for children to allow themselves to rest. The children must clearly understand what the expectations are at this time: stay calm, go to the bathroom, get a favorite soft toy, help put down a mat or cot, and so forth. When necessary, remind children with a calm and convincing voice of the instructions, without inducing guilt. A poster where children can see what they have to do to prepare for nap is helpful, provided children are reminded to look at it.

- It may take up to forty-five minutes to help children prepare for naptime and fall asleep. For the first part of the year, repeat the routine in exactly the same way. After that, gradually introduce small variations at the beginning of naptime as necessary, depending on the children's receptivity.

- Direct preschoolers to start lying down on their cots/mats earlier, around 12:30 or 1:00 PM. Unfortunately, some centers start nap even earlier, around noon or even 11:30 AM, without taking into account the children's signs of sleepiness.

- Eliminate sources of sensory stimulation: light; radio, television, or traffic noise; movement; loud voices (including adult voices); a high number of children in the same room; and, in a home child care setting, all the normal household noises.

- Place a sign on the door asking visitors to knock instead of ringing the bell. Lower the volume of the telephone ringer.

- Install cots/mats and bedding with the children's cooperation. Ensure a minimum personal space of about two feet between each mattress/cot (this also serves to minimize the spread of infection). As much as possible, keep children's allotted spaces the same every day. However, children can take turns sleeping in some special space; for example, under a table or in a favorite corner. In home child care situations, the educator's own child may prefer to sleep in his own room rather than in the common room.

- If you provide child care in your home, you must find a safe sleeping place for younger children. Large beds are not appropriate.

- Let fresh air into the room after lunch and before naptime to ensure good air quality. Avoid drafts, cold floors, and fans directly on the children.

- Respect children's comforting habits at the beginning of naptime: rocking, rhythmic movements, twisting a hair strand, auto-erotic stimulation (masturbation), playing with the hands, cuddling with a soft toy. These habits are healthy for children as long as they are safe, hygienic, and do not disturb other children. Transition objects should be easy to wash and to store in children's individual cubbies. Try to keep these comforting items—a special blanket or toy—at the center as much as possible. Without them, children will often be too stressed to benefit from a nap. To encourage children to prepare quickly for nap, it is best to give them their comfort item only when they are lying down on their mat or cot.

- Suggest to the children that they self-massage their face, hands, or feet, according to their preference. Massaging children's backs should be done only occasionally, not as a daily routine. When massaging a child's back, observe her verbal and nonverbal reactions, since sensitivity and the need to be touched differ from one child to another at this time of the day. Some children do not like this type of contact, and it may even prevent them from falling asleep. It is better to help children to relax by themselves, rather than conditioning them to fall asleep with the direct intervention of an adult. If you judge

that it is necessary for you to help a child by stroking her, avoid crouching or bending. Rather, sit comfortably, with your back supported, or ask for the help of those older than five.

- Watch that a peaceful atmosphere is maintained by moving softly, speaking with a low voice, or singing a lullaby. Do not disturb the children by speaking loudly or blaming the children for anything, or by chatting among educators. Adult chitchat has no place in a child care center, especially during naptime.

- Ensure direct and constant supervision of children for the duration of nap. Conform to any government-mandated child-educator ratio. How could a single educator evacuate thirty children from a room in an emergency?

> *Enforce safety precautions at all times. This means during naptime, preparing for naptime, getting up from nap, and storing equipment after nap. If children are allowed to take off their shoes, watch out for slippery socks that could lead to a fall, and pay attention to choking risks posed by children's jewelry items or decorative buttons on children's clothes or soft toys.*

- Ensure that an educator familiar to the children is there during the nap ritual to help children feel secure.

- In cooperation with other team members and parents, plan and implement a program for children who create disturbances during naptime (excessive autoerotic stimulation, crisis, and overexcitement). If a child disturbs naptime often, one solution could be to place her with another group for a while. This might alleviate the child's behavior problem while giving the educator a respite.

- If possible, lie down yourself on an available cot or mat to rest a little while watching over the group. With ten to eleven hours of work a day, home child care educators need to rest during naptime by sitting on a comfortable chair while they supervise the children.

- Use naptime to fill in children's journals while maintaining adequate supervision.

> *It is important to communicate to parents problems that might arise during naptime (nervousness, change of sleep pattern, unusual crying). Informed parents will be able to help educators understand what is happening and also do some follow-up at home.*

5.7 Getting up from nap

After a nap, children need some time to wake up completely before they start new activities, preferably calm ones. It is best for them to wake up spontaneously. Within reason, children should be left to get up by themselves, according to their individual rhythms. "Don't expect all children to wake up at the same time from their naps" (Brickman and Taylor 1991, 138). Some children need help to wake up completely, find their personal belongings, and store their mat or cot. If a child needs to be awakened for a valid reason, it is best to do it progressively using soft words and actions. The child can be given several options—get up alone, accept help, start with a particular task—to get his cooperation.

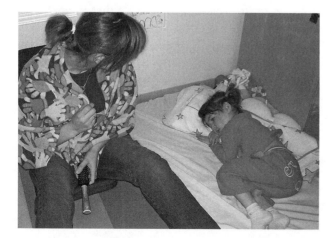

Staggered awakening allows you to give each child some individual attention and help. Do not let children sleep past 4:00 PM unless an exceptional situation occurs, as this may disturb night sleep.

5.8 Other factors that affect nap and rest time

Various extrinsic or intrinsic factors influence the quality of a naptime. Box 5.4 gives some examples. Take time to study them closely.

BOX 5.4 **Factors influencing nap quality**

- Bad habits used to initiate sleep, such as the need for a back massage, the need for complete silence, and so forth.

- Seasonal changes, which can affect metabolism and, indirectly, sleep needs (lack of sun, temperature changes, heat or cold). For example, heat and sun in summer lower the sleep requirements of children and adults (Thirion and Challamel 1999).

- Environmental conditions that positively or negatively influence sleep, such as room temperature, air quality, comfort (mat too small, cold floor, no blanket), noise, and personal space.

- Uncomfortable decorations or stuffing on children's clothes. This is also true of clothes that are too tight. Advise parents to choose comfortable clothes for naptime.

- Individual temperament and genetic characteristics (aggressive tendencies, light or heavy sleeper, late or early sleeper, and so forth).

- Individual experiences (mat or cot is associated with punishment or abandonment, fear of the dark).

- Period of adaptation to the center or irregular attendance (which makes acceptance of the nap routine difficult), the presence of an unfamiliar substitute, physical problems such as a blocked nose, anxiety due to parents' divorce or a planned stay at the hospital, and so forth.

- Ingestion of foods with a high sugar and fat content that stimulate and overload the body, as well as render digestion more difficult. At the other end of the spectrum, hunger may prevent sleep and relaxation.

- Insufficient rest and relaxation periods during the day that impair the natural sleeping rhythm. Excessive fatigue and overexertion can play havoc with children's normal sleeping patterns. This is why quiet relaxation periods every ninety minutes or so are recommended.

- Certain medications that induce restlessness (antibiotics, bronchodilators, decongestants, cough syrup), whether these medications have been taken at the center or not. Parents should be told to broach this subject with the child's doctor. It is important that educators be informed of the side effects of any medication a child may be taking.

Children who have difficulty falling asleep, letting go, or relaxing need to feel adult empathy. Remember your own relaxation difficulties as an adult when confronted by children with the same difficulties.

5.9 Games to introduce rest time

Once the adaptation period (which can last a few months) to the naptime routine at the center is over, new elements can be added to break the monotony. Obviously, these elements should be geared toward making nap or relaxation efficient and beneficial for all. Box 5.5 provides some suggestions.

BOX 5.5 **Suggestions to facilitate nap**

- Read books with stories that facilitate naptime. Some stories even present ideas to help reconcile children with the idea of taking a nap.

- On the ceiling of the room, affix shiny, personalized stars that watch over each child during nap. Stars can be made and decorated by the children.

- If a child has difficulty listening quietly to a story before nap, give her the option either to listen to the story with the group or to look quietly at a book on her own cot.

- Use a ball to give children lying on their cot/mat a small massage. Make sure the effect is calming, not stimulating. Some children do not like this type of touch. Always pay attention to the child's reaction, and take it into account.

- Suggest light stretching exercises to do while lying on the cot/mat.

- Hum melodies softly instead of singing songs. Words are more stimulating than calming.

- Play soothing music in the background. If you opt for background music from a tape/CD, select music without words, since words stimulate the brain. Avoid sad or depressing music. Play music very softly and stop it after twenty to thirty minutes to avoid fatiguing the ear, even if children are asleep. Silence is better. It is not a good idea to listen to music on the radio since it is difficult to control. It is better to play humming voices, nature sounds (such as the sound of water flowing or soft waves), bird songs, or cricket sounds.

- Pay a visit to children who are calmly lying on their cots, carrying a puppet that is going to give each calm child a little pat. This may encourage other children to calm down.

- Circulate between beds with a flashlight. Illuminate the body of each child to "make him or her sleep."

- Improvise a story in which children transform their mat/cot into an imaginary train that takes a trip through fascinating and reassuring places.

- Use calm songs to help the children wake up.

6

Dressing and Undressing

CHAPTER CONTENTS

6.1 Equipment and organization

6.2 Duration

6.3 Upon arrival and departure and when going outside
and coming back in

6.4 Factors that make dressing and undressing easier

A. Adapted clothing

B. Adapted tasks

6.5 Little games

Dressing and undressing (putting on a coat, unbuttoning a vest, differentiating the inside from the outside of a sweater, putting on gloves) are simple tasks performed automatically by adults, but for a two-year-old, these basic actions represent a major challenge that must be overcome by systematic learning. This requires much effort and repetition. Only around age six or seven can the child execute with ease the art of getting dressed and undressed in a relatively short time.

In educational settings, there are numerous activities that require dressing and undressing: arrivals and departures, before and after outdoor play, before and after nap (when shoes must be taken off and put back on). These require a lot of time and concentration, especially with younger children. Children must acquire specific skills to put on pants or socks, button a sweater, zipper a coat, put the right foot into the right shoe, tie the knot on a hat, put on an apron, and so forth. Through constant repetition they progressively acquire autonomy.

Health and safety as well as the children's sense of well-being are also concerns during dressing and

undressing. Several conditions must exist concurrently to make dressing and undressing a pleasant routine.

6.1 Equipment and organization

As with other situations, space and the materials used have a big influence on dressing and undressing activities. Notably, the location, size, and organization of the changing area are important. For example, a changing area close to the main room as well as to the outside exit minimizes waiting times and facilitates group movements (both of which are frequently a source of children's restlessness). If the changing area is in a crowded area, there needs to be at least enough space for children to dress and undress without bumping into passersby. If this is not the case (and even though it might be somewhat inconvenient), have the children dress and undress in their homeroom, bringing the children their clothes (unless the room is equipped with hooks for the children's clothes). A changing area big enough to accommodate a group of children and their parents is ideal because it allows dressing and undressing tasks to be performed calmly. Putting on boots or a coat takes some room. Also, a hallway between the changing area and the outside protects children from temperature extremes.

The changing area should be equipped with individual cubbies that are large enough to allow damp clothing to dry; benches or chairs to facilitate putting on and taking off shoes or boots; a table to place babies on while they are being dressed or undressed; and an antiskid, easy-to-clean floor.

Children need individual hooks to hang up coats and other clothing, and enough space to store boots or shoes, as well as a backpack. An additional shelf is needed to store hats, caps, and mittens. A cubby is often the only place that children have for their personal belongings. Therefore, children should be able to decorate their cubbies with pictures or drawings.

Personal belongings should be identified with a sturdy label. Parents will probably need to be reminded to identify all their children's clothing. There should be a place (box, shelf) designated as the lost-and-found area that is easily accessible to parents. During cold months, children should leave a pair of shoes at the center.

Parents should have easy access to the center. Boot covers or slippers allow them to walk around the center without making the floors wet when there is rain or snow. Some centers require parents to wear boot covers.

6.2 Duration

The time allotted for dressing and undressing has a big influence on the success of this activity. If the allotted time is too short, the children will feel pressured, stressed, or incompetent, and if it is too long, they become impatient. Of course, beginners will need help and practice; this will take some time. Ideally, children should neither feel pressured nor have to wait.

To encourage cooperation and minimize time loss, children should be reminded, in clear terms, of the expectations for dressing and undressing. "Put on your snow pants, Tony; then I will help you button them up." "Alexia, I expect you to place your coat on the right hook today." Remind children of the next activity as a way to motivate them. "Ahmad, when you finish getting dressed, we will take out the tricycles from the shed. I will need your help." Children forget at times why they must get dressed. A reminder may be necessary to get them to cooperate.

6.3 Upon arrival and departure and when going outside and coming back in

When children arrive at or leave the center, ask for parents' cooperation in undressing or dressing their children so that educators remain available to the other children and their parents. Departure time is especially important for exchanges between staff and parents. It is important that parents have a clear understanding of what is expected of them and at what point they need to take care of their child. There is nothing worse than having confusion and misunderstanding occur at the end of the day, when everyone—parents, staff, and children—are tired and prone to tension.

For five-year-olds, the dressing and undressing routine is generally easy. Their motor skills and their need for increased autonomy facilitate this activity, even if an educator's support is required to motivate and guide them. In cold weather, the older children may even help the younger ones get dressed. Their role, it must be stressed, is not to dress the younger ones but to support learning.

When the floor of the entryway is wet, it is preferable for children to change into their shoes elsewhere to avoid soaking their socks.

When children get dressed or undressed, they can also go to the bathroom or have a drink of water, if there is a bathroom close by. This reduces crowding in the changing area. Moreover, when children are dressed, they should be able to go out in small groups with an educator.

When preparing for outdoor play, some children can be given the responsibility of carrying the materials to be taken outside: balls, skipping ropes, shovels, chalk, and so forth. When children see these play materials, they are motivated to get dressed quickly.

6.4 Factors that make dressing and undressing easier

Getting dressed or undressed can take many forms, depending on the children, weather, group interaction, and so forth. The factors at play are not always easy to control. However, there are some factors that can be controlled or manipulated.

A. ADAPTED CLOTHING

It is easier and faster to get dressed and undressed if clothing is safe and without belts or laces/cords. Everything is easier if children wear a turtleneck or muffler instead of a scarf, if they have boots and shoes with Velcro fasteners, and if clothes are not too loose or too tight. Each season has its specific clothes: in winter, a hat to shield the head from cold and a light sweater to avoid overheating and perspiring; in summer, waterproof boots for rainy weather, and so forth.

> *Set a good example by dressing for the temperature and the activity. It is difficult to require children to wear a hat if you are not wearing one. Remember that children are influenced more by behavior than by words. Also, if you are dressed warmly you will not ask children to come in early because you are cold yourself.*

One-piece clothing, such as overalls, might be difficult to put on. Pants with an elastic waistband, zippers with rings or handles for easier grabbing, and Velcro shoe straps simplify tasks. Inform parents of the types of clothing that simplify dressing and undressing tasks. They will usually cooperate by dressing their children in practical clothes.

B. ADAPTED TASKS

Since getting undressed is easier than getting dressed, focus on the former task with the beginners. "Undressing is the first stage of autonomy related to getting dressed" (Martin, Poulin, and Falardeau 1992, 155). When children are learning to use the toilet, they sometimes enjoy getting undressed. They need to be told to just take off their pants.

The dressing and undressing routine varies greatly from one child to the next. Some are not used to performing this task, since their parents do it for them. Two-year-olds can remove their shoes if the shoelaces are undone. However, they cannot tie the laces themselves. This is a task they will be able to manage around age six. With a few exceptions, children will have learned to get dressed and undressed without help by school age. See Table 6.1 for a list of motor skills required for dressing

and undressing and at what age most children master those skills.

Assist children learning to get dressed by describing the tasks to be done. You may even rhyme these descriptions to make them attractive. Younger children must be encouraged to cooperate. For example, put a child's arm into a sleeve first and then ask the child to extend her arm. Sliding the sleeve over the child's arm becomes easier. Show the zipper on the child's garment to the child and encourage her to zip it up. Unfasten the first button and let the child unfasten the next one, and so forth. Young children learn how to dress and undress in the same way they learn other fine-motor skills—with repetition and encouragement.

6.5 Little games

Note: These games should stimulate children to get dressed and not distract them from this task.

- Issue a challenge. "Can you put on your boots by yourself today?" "Do you remember where to hang up your coat?" "Can you do it yourself?"
- Play "Simon says." "Simon says to put on boots. Put on mittens."
- Color game. "Put on a piece of clothing with blue in it." "Put on a piece of clothing with patterns."
- Reward children when they have finished getting dressed or undressed. For example, give them a sticker or stamp their hands.

Remember not to penalize slower children. Each child will get the reward once dressed.

- Post drawings or pictures of clothes to put on, especially in cold climates when there are lots of clothes to put on: sweaters, snowpants, boots, hats, scarves, coats, mittens.

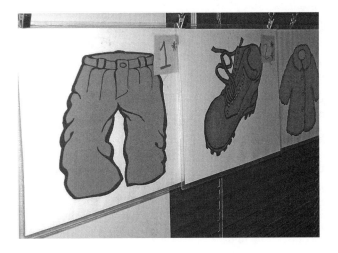

- Describe what each child is doing. "I see Nadia putting on her coat. I also see Manuel, who is ready to go out."
- Sing a song reminding the children of the name and the order of clothing to put on.
- If you live in a cold climate, before coming back inside on a snowy day, perform a "shaking dance" to shake the snow from clothing.
- Make little games available for children who are finished dressing so they have something to do while waiting for the others. First, ask them to sit along a wall, and then distribute the play material.

TABLE 6.1 **Motor skills required for dressing and undressing tasks in children**

	Shoes	Clothes	Suggestions
TWO YEARS **Undressing easier than dressing.**	Able to push foot into shoe with help. Able to take off shoes if untied. Able to take off boots without assistance.	Able to find sleeve or pant leg and push arm or leg into it. Able to lower and raise underwear. Able to take off some clothes with help. Able to partially pull up zipper.	Help children identify clothes and their use. Give ample opportunities for dressing up during dramatic play to practice skills such as pulling a zipper up, pushing an arm into sleeve, etc. Allow trial and error. Play games: The arm enters the tunnel (sleeve), etc.
THREE YEARS **Hand movements are more precise.** **Children show an increased desire for autonomy.**	May still put on wrong shoe. Able to put on boots without assistance. Able to untie shoelaces and unbuckle sandals. Able to put on shoes with Velcro fasteners without help.	Able to undress. Able to put on sweaters and shirts with help. May still put on clothes inside out or front to back. Can unbutton if buttons are in front or on the side. Better at knowing which order to put on clothes. Able to unzipper clothes.	Position yourself on the side or behind the child when teaching the proper techniques. Remind children to put on coats before putting on mittens. Offer play materials that make children practice buttoning skills. Give children time to get dressed. Teach terms such as *forward, inside out, put on, take off,* and so forth.
FOUR YEARS **Fine-motor skills improve.**	Starts to tie laces. Able to buckle sandals.	Able to detect inside/outside and front/back in clothes. Able to get dressed with simple clothes. Able to pull up zipper. Can do two things at the same time. For example, talk and undress. Able to attach fasteners.	Introduce tying and lacing games.
FIVE YEARS **Speed and precision improve.**	Can put the right foot in the right shoe most of the time.	Able to dress and undress well. Able to fully pull up zipper.	Encourage children to help each other. (This supposes that both parties agree!)
SIX YEARS AND OLDER **At ease getting dressed.**	Able to tie shoelaces. Able to distinguish left from right shoe.	Able to accomplish dressing tasks faster. Still needs help to fasten buttons located at the neck, the wrists, and the back.	

7

Tidying and Cleaning Up

CHAPTER CONTENTS

7.1 A practical storage system
   A. The area and the equipment
   B. Getting children to help
   C. Tidying the outdoor space
   D. Labeling

7.2 Cleaning up

7.3 How you can encourage tidy-up and cleanup
   A. Planning the display of games and materials
   B. Having realistic expectations
   C. Fostering learning
   D. Giving advance warning
   E. Managing time
   F. Providing positive reinforcement
   G. Letting children bear the consequences
   H. Being active
   I. Encouraging ongoing tidy-up

7.4 Tidy-up and clean-up games
   A. A job for everyone
   B. Three cheers for creativity!
   C. A bit of complicity
   D. Dusting
   E. Counting
   F. Magical vacuum cleaner
   G. What do you want to put away?
   H. Music time!
   I. Parallel play for the end of cleanup
   J. A challenge for you
   K. Timing
   L. Relay cleanup
   M. One demonstration equals a thousand explanations
   N. Speaking toys
   O. Ways to move around
   P. "Simon says"

7.5 Clean-up songs

All early childhood educators will agree: tidying and cleaning up are not among children's favorite activities. Some educators even dread tidying and cleaning time. They see the group of children grow restless and disorganized, breaking the harmony gained during the previous play period. In an early childhood education program, these routine activities are performed many times daily, and they are very time consuming. The key is to find ways to turn them into fully satisfying transitions. It's necessary to understand the challenges of tidying and cleaning up in order to turn them into beneficial activities for children and educators alike.

One of the secrets of a good early childhood education program is the organization of effective tidy-up transitions. This often requires some thinking and several trials to find the best organization and storage solutions for equipment and materials, whether they are used daily or only occasionally.

The first step is to plan an efficient material storage and search system, while encouraging children's autonomy (to a degree appropriate to their level of development). Second, this system must be implemented with flexibility to minimize the stress inherent in tidying and cleaning up. Specific behaviors on the part of educators may impair the harmonious accomplishment of the task: asking children to hurry up to meet the demands of the program, spending a lot of energy and time on discipline, getting impatient when difficulties arise, implying that it is better to hurry up to do something more important. Smooth transitions can be encouraged by adopting a flexible schedule that allows a few extra minutes for tidying and cleaning up. This shows the importance of work well done and of tidying up for the group. Introducing this task to the children as a form of play will make this transition easier and will teach valuable skills.

Once you've assessed your storage needs, develop an action plan adapted to your particular program to organize a safe and efficient storage space. This requires creativity. In a home child care setting, ingenuity is required to prevent the stored materials from invading the space where the family lives at night and on the weekend. You might consider placing the storage boxes behind the couch, piling the cushions above a closet, using moveable containers, setting up a dressing area away from the entrance closet, and so forth. In a school setting, where there may be only one room allocated for the child care program, lack of storage space may be a serious problem. A storage strategy is required to simplify the many daily occurrences of tidy-up time.

7.1 A practical storage system

The success of tidying and cleaning activities inevitably depends on the area where these activities take place as well as the type of materials used. Obstacles that hinder tidying and cleaning activities include a small play area, difficult-to-reach storage for outdoor play, or hard-to-maintain furniture. Since the quality of the center depends to a large degree on the level of organization and storage, it is vital to identify the conditions that lead to well-organized routines.

A. THE AREA AND THE EQUIPMENT

The setup of the area must be conducive to keeping things tidy: cubbies and hooks for children's clothes and personal belongings (discussed in chapter 6); cabinets with moveable shelves; low cabinets placed against a wall or used as partitions; and storage modules on casters, which makes them easy to push from one room to another (the casters should have a locking mechanism to prevent the module from unintended movement). Any mobile storage equipment with compartments and drawers (such as sturdy and stackable plastic storage boxes with drawers) is always very useful. For language

activities, useful storage solutions are book display shelves at child level, transparent plastic envelopes in which to insert figurines, and Velcro fasteners tacked onto the wall to hold puppets. For artwork, it is important to have a drying area, a storage place for unfinished work, and a recycling bin for paper.

Home- or center-based programs may care for children of various ages. Therefore, play material must be organized for children at various developmental stages.

If a toy box is used, remove the hinge to prevent children from catching their fingers in it. Boxes and trunks should not be too deep. If they are fairly shallow, children will not try to empty them when looking for a toy. Old laundry detergent boxes with the tops cut off are ideal for storing magazines and catalogs for cutout activities and collages. Plastic mesh boxes and laundry baskets allow children to see contents easily. However, a finger or hand may get caught in an opening, so choose the plastic mesh carefully. The openings must be large enough for a finger to go through without getting stuck, and small enough to prevent the whole hand from passing through. In an early childhood education program, space and equipment must be safe in all respects. Remember, children's physical well-being is the first priority. Box 7.1 lists some factors to consider when choosing and organizing storage.

BOX 7.1 **Basic elements to consider for storage**

- Safe play material that is easy for children to manipulate.
- Materials within easy reach, without necessitating a lot of bending or stretching.
- Solid low shelving that is clearly labeled.
- Shelves and hooks at child level.
- Chairs that are easily moveable by children.
- Cabinets and drawers that are easy to open and use symbols to clearly identify their contents.
- Transparent plastic containers without holes that are easy to handle, open, and move, and whose contents are easy to identify.

- Easy-to-clean containers, cubbies, and storage equipment (yes, they must be cleaned from time to time).
- Storage that keeps dangerous, fragile, and expensive material out of the reach of children unless under close adult supervision.
- Storage for software and compact discs that keeps them safe and dust free.

A well-organized storage system prolongs the life span of material and allows children to take the initiative in organizing their own play material. If they can easily identify the table game they are looking for, if they are able to take a tricycle out easily, or if they can find the paper they need to draw on, children will meet their own needs and increase their autonomy. Ensure that children correctly store the material used during play by encouraging them to find it, move it, use it, and put it back in its proper place. A well-designed environment will foster children's feeling of competence and help them take responsibility—essential elements in the development of self-esteem.

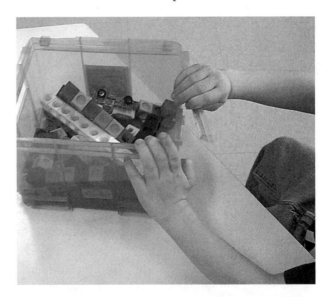

A room organized in a logical manner encourages children to tidy up and helps the educator feel in control of the group. It also contributes to building a safe and pleasant environment for all.

Obviously, grouping similar items in the same area—blocks in the block corner, books in the reading corner, art material in the art area—follows certain logic. However, in the context of a democratic pedagogy, where it is desirable for materials to have multiple uses (for example, the availability of playdough in both the art corner and the kitchen corner), there may be an advantage in grouping various types of materials together. If objects with a common function, such as beads, pieces of straw, and strands of wool, are placed on the same shelf, children may be inspired to make necklaces and bracelets. However, children will be less likely to associate ideas and create new games if these materials are dispersed through the room—particularly if they are stored out of sight and out of reach. Consider the following: If you place a few picture books on a multicultural topic close to records of ethnic songs, this new association of materials might prompt children to listen to the music since it is connected to visual elements. Stimulating children's creativity is often a matter of simply modifying the organization of materials.

The tidy-up routine is the perfect occasion to increase children's level of respect for objects and equipment in their environment. Above all, avoid piling up material on shelves and mixing objects in boxes. For example, if children see all the dress-up props in a heap, they will have difficulty recognizing them and will not be interested in playing with them. Another problem is the crowding of tables and the floor, often with objects that have no place in a child care environment. Store such material in its proper place, and take it out at the right time.

B. GETTING CHILDREN TO HELP

For a child, tidying and cleaning up often means the end of pleasurable play, and that may be very frustrating. Getting children interested in these tasks is an important challenge for the educator. Take the opportunity to make children aware of the advantage of having a tidy and clean space. The tidy-up routine should allow children to acquire a responsible attitude toward material and equipment according to their level of development. For example, you may encourage children to report any lost or broken material. You may also emphasize the disadvantages of untidiness (difficulty in finding play items, lost pieces of a puzzle preventing its completion, damage to books that are left lying around, danger of falling over objects left on the floor) or of dirtiness (food scraps on the floor that allow the growth of bacteria and pose a danger to health). Occasionally, you may present an interesting story to raise children's awareness of this. Remember that children get a taste for cleaning up little by little. Above all, the examples set by adults play a major role in children's learning. These examples must be coherent and convincing for the children if they are to be effective.

Children must understand the rules for using material as well as the consequences for failing to follow these rules. In school child care centers, rules may be designed and implemented in cooperation with the children.

C. TIDYING THE OUTDOOR SPACE

Outdoor storage facilities should be as strategically organized as indoor ones. Storage should be planned so that at the end of the day outdoor materials are stored in a shed or brought back indoors. It is important to have either mobile storage or a shed that is easy to access and functional to shelter material from bad weather and prevent theft. The

sandbox should have a sturdy, weatherproof top to minimize maintenance. Carts with wheels are handy for children to use to carry and store play materials. Good planning will alleviate the heavy load of the educator during outdoor play and make overall tidying up more enjoyable.

Outdoor tidying up and maintenance of the yard are two wonderful opportunities to introduce children to issues of environmental protection and ecology. Taking care of a tree, putting refuse in a garbage can, and raking dead leaves and preparing them for mulching are a few tasks that will expose children to the idea of taking care of their environment.

Security of the outdoor play area must be a priority at all times. Consult the appropriate regulations on outdoor safety.

D. LABELING

An effective classification system is designed to allow for the visual identification of all items in containers, cassettes, and boxes and of all areas of the room (science area, shelves for table games, and so forth). Efficient labels are attractive, explicit, secure, and durable. They can display pictures, drawings, illustrations, cutouts from catalogs or fliers, imprints of the enclosed objects, or symbols. They make it possible for children to identify where the actual objects must be stored. For young readers, a simple word written on a container may be sufficient. For very young children, an actual object glued to the storage box (for instance, a felt pen affixed to the felt-pen box) is the simplest method for identifying and sorting materials. When preschoolers show an interest in letters and words, stimulate their curiosity by writing the name of the object next to the corresponding picture.

An effective method for sorting play materials helps prevent the loss of pieces of play material, a common problem in child care centers. For instance, coding the back of puzzle pieces with a colored dot for each puzzle is an effective solution. This system is a sure way to help children place all pieces from a particular puzzle in the proper box. When a piece is missing from a form board, draw an X in the space of the missing piece and avoid a useless search.

7.2 Cleaning up

If systematic organization is a major characteristic of a healthy and harmonious early childhood education program, cleanliness also plays an important role. While an aseptic environment is not the goal, educators still have to consider cleanliness as carefully as tidiness.

Nothing replaces soap and water for cleaning surfaces and removing microorganisms. However, a number of objects and surfaces must be sanitized after cleanup. Child care center regulations usually state clear guidelines pertaining to sanitizing. Obviously, children are not to participate in this because it involves dangerous chemical cleaning products. However, children have the opportunity to participate in other cleaning tasks.

What child does not enjoy the responsibility of wiping up the table after lunch or of washing the paintbrushes in the sink? These tasks quickly become a fascinating water play. And what about sweeping the floor after cutting paper or washing the dishes after cooking? Children feel proud to accomplish adult tasks, especially when you go out of your way to thank them and emphasize the importance of their actions. "These tasks, satisfying in themselves, gain even greater value in the eyes of the children when the educator emphasizes their utility for the whole group" (Hendrick 1988, 237).

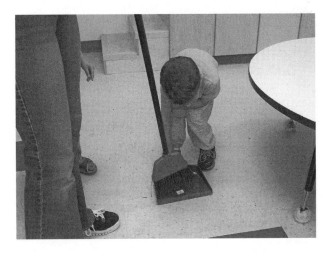

Many tasks require the cooperation of several children, which has the advantage of enhancing their social skills. For example, one child may sweep up paper cuttings with a broom while another holds the dustpan, or one child may wash the dishes in the house play area while a classmate dries them.

Consider playdough, which often leaves tables and floors covered with bits and crumbs. Before children remove their aprons, they can place the playdough or clay in containers, then remove the crumbs from their hands and the table with brown paper towels or with a modeling tool. This helps avoid plugged drains when crumbs find their way into the sink. Cleaning is completed by washing the tables with soapy water and wiping them off. Wash hands before going to the next activity.

As with playdough, fingerpainting is generally greeted with wild enthusiasm. Why deprive them of it! Whether with a commercial product, a home recipe, a mixture of cornstarch and water, or even shaving cream, fingerpainting can be done directly on the table with the hands—children love it. At the end, clean hands and surfaces in the same manner as the playdough activity. Remove excess paint with a paper towel. This step clearly announces the end of the activity. It also reduces the length of hand-washing time and overall cleaning, and it is easy on the drains. While children are washing their hands at the sink (or in a pail of water if the sinks are too far away), you can finish washing the table.

Educators have to clean tables several times a day (before and after a snack or after a messy activity). Generally, a chemical cleaner is used to wipe off the tables.

> *When cleaning tables, to prevent spray mist from drifting onto nearby children, spray the chemical directly onto the wiping cloth. Providers should protect children from inhaling invisible droplets of chemicals or otherwise coming in contact with them. Safeguarding children's health is an early childhood educator's responsibility.*

7.3 How you can encourage tidy-up and cleanup

It is important to make use of everything that can make tidying and cleaning tasks easy and enjoyable processes. In addition to employing an effective storage system and room arrangement, educators should foster children's acquisition of skills so children can participate in transition activities. This section focuses on direct teacher interventions, actions, and words that determine the level of satisfaction gained from tidying and cleaning activities.

A. PLANNING THE DISPLAY OF GAMES AND MATERIALS

We may think that a large number of toys displayed on the floor or on a table will increase children's interest. However, this is not the case. When children have too many choices of play materials, or when the display is disorderly, children often feel confused. They may have difficulty finding what they want and setting up their play. Instead of focusing on quantity, focus on variety and on the relevance of materials to the children's interests and abilities. Give them the opportunity to make choices by displaying the toys in an attractive way.

It is useless to take out everything day after day in the hope of fostering quality play. Children love novelty, so regular turnover of play objects keeps them interested. Moreover, exchanging play materials among groups or borrowing materials from a toy library brings a variety to children's play without overspending on and overcrowding a space that is often already restricted.

B. HAVING REALISTIC EXPECTATIONS

Although they can be enjoyable, tidying and cleaning are nevertheless tasks imposed on children by adults. When the time comes to clean up or tidy up, children usually do not say they want to clean up; rather, they voice their desire to continue playing. Do not expect overwhelming spontaneous enthusiasm from the children—even less so if the task is disheartening. It is normal for them not to enjoy tidying or cleaning up, since they do not understand the reason for this activity. Understanding follows the various stages of intellectual maturation. For example, because children over the age of four have a better awareness than younger children of time and of hunger, they will rush through cleaning and washing their hands so they can eat.

With adult perseverance and tact, and through repeated experience, children will grasp the purpose of tidying and clean-up activities.

Children go through a healthy stage of self-affirmation. When they are at this stage, presenting tidy-up time in an authoritarian and dogmatic way is sure to lead to useless confrontations. It is better to use a strategic approach. For example, children can be given the choice between two objects to put away, or the task can be framed in terms of a personal challenge of some sort, taking into account the child's resistance while leading her diplomatically to accomplish the requested task.

Two-year-old children are natural "movers"—they like to move objects from one place to another. Take advantage of this desire by making a game out of appropriately storing materials instead of just moving them around. With reasonable expectations, you can create a relaxed climate during the tidying and cleaning transition period, even if those activities are unpopular with most children.

Having realistic expectations about children's abilities and motivation levels also means taking into account such factors as the various energy levels during the day, the critical periods in a child's life, the adaptation process of a newcomer, a two-year-old's opposition, an eight-year-old's need to argue, upcoming holidays, and even those days when everybody seems restless or in a bad mood.

The ability to adapt to a situation is one of the most important competencies required by the early childhood education profession.

Although it is better not to repeat instructions too often, they are essential to learning the rules necessary to life in an educational setting. Nonetheless, authoritarian orders accompanied by long explanations, recriminations, comparisons, and threats are detrimental. To reactivate a child's brain to what needs to be done at clean-up time, use methods adapted to her level of development that will produce positive feelings in her. Children learn through pleasure. As much as possible, tidying up must be turned into a game instead of a chore. See Box 7.2.

BOX 7.2 Methods to help children participate in tidying and cleaning activities

- Initiate short activities that end with a brief transitional time of tidy-up. Children will be successful and proud. (Two- and three-year-olds.)

- Get children to find solutions to their problems, including disinterest, lack of attention and focus, and so forth. (Ages five and older.)

- Surprise the group by using humor in certain situations. "The woodworking area needs help!" (All ages.)

- Give responsibilities to children so they feel grown up. (Three- to eight-year-olds.)

- Encourage a child to clean up by calling his name. (All ages.)

- Have children make a poster that reminds them with pictures or words of the cleaning steps after a messy activity. (Five- to eight-year-olds.)

- An activity that takes five minutes to set up should not necessitate more than five minutes of cleanup. Knowing this, do not be frustrated when you see children are only interested in an activity for five minutes. This applies especially to children who prefer short activities and, consequently, short cleanup.

To counter a child's lack of interest in tidying up, stay close to her at the beginning, and make comments such as, "Antonia, what pretend clothes will you put away first?" "What do you want us to do to put the blocks back in their place? Count them, or play photographer?" "Look at this drawer, Alexandra. Can you see what should go inside?" Children with attention difficulties who regularly get lost in their own imaginary world need a little nudge to get out of it and start putting away their belongings or their play materials. Patience is the rule when guiding these children through tidy-up steps. This takes energy and time, but it is well worth it.

> Your approach has to be realistic. This means understanding the child's point of view and learning to see through the child's eyes. It also means taking into account the child's stage of development, his disposition, the family context, and so forth. A realistic approach will help prevent difficulties that may arise while tidying or cleaning up.

C. FOSTERING LEARNING

Despite their lack of popularity, tidy-up and clean-up activities provide valuable opportunities for child development. In the area of socio-affective development, children may learn to take care of their environment, respect materials, become responsible, and, especially, help one another. You can consciously promote this development in the way you address the children: "Who would be nice enough to help Jina put the beads back in the box?" "Thank you, Jamal, for giving a hand to Fiona in the block corner." "Ana, I see you are taking good care of the pencils by putting them back in the box." "Pascal, what have you forgotten?"

Sorting and classifying objects, counting them, finding their proper place, orienting oneself in space, and decoding a symbol on a label are all exercises that promote cognitive development. Consider skills such as spatial organization, ordering, deduction, and the ability to solve problems. Asking children to store toys by matching the symbol on the box to the symbol on the shelf, or asking them to group materials and toys according to their function (dramatic play props), color (blue containers in the house corner), or size (small blocks, large blocks, and so on) encourages classification and memory skills.

In the area of motor development, fine-motor skills are honed through activities such as washing paintbrushes, closing lids, screwing tops on stamp pads and storing them in their box, and folding the bedding and placing it in the cubbie.

Verbal communication development is assisted through the correct identification of objects, the use of new vocabulary, verbal exchanges among children or with an educator, and dramatic play and songs to facilitate tasks.

Being successful increases self-esteem, which is part of affective development. Do not be afraid of repetition with two- and three-year-old children. By repeating a particular experience, by going over the same process again and again, children in this age group become progressively more confident. This will facilitate the next tidy-up activity. If children get tired of repeating the same clean-up games, they will let you know.

Early childhood educators need to take every occasion to practice tidy-up. Besides the cleanup associated with the end of play periods, encourage tidy-up and clean-up tasks associated with daily routines (such as piling up empty cups after a snack, placing mats in the closet, or sweeping the patio floor before serving snacks outside) and with special events and outdoor play.

> Tidy-up activities are golden opportunities to encourage children's whole development. Educators have the responsibility of exploiting these opportunities.

D. GIVING ADVANCE WARNING

When children are given advance notice of tidy-up or cleanup, they are more inclined to react positively. If you give them a warning a few minutes before the end of an activity, they will get ready in a natural way to start the next activity and to start tidying up. Beyond the simple verbal instruction, "It is time to clean up," which the children may eventually cease to hear, visual clues (a light blinking, a sign with the hand) or auditory clues (a song, the sounding of a triangle, pleasant music) are effective ways to announce clean-up time. Older children who know how to tell time can be told that tidy-up time will start when the long hand reaches a particular number. When cleanup and tidy-up take place at the same time an activity is winding down, remind a child who has forgotten the directions: "What do you need to do, Luis, when you've finished eating? Yes, that's it. You need to empty your plate and take it to the cart."

E. MANAGING TIME

Time constraints increase the stress level of children. Plan enough time to have an unhurried transition and show flexibility. Good time management will guarantee a successful experience. In some educational settings, it is noticeable that children are pressured by a schedule, the purpose of which is mainly to meet the educators' needs. Here are three examples: getting children ready for naptime in a hurry, so educators can take their break; hastily putting away the outdoor material to facilitate the handover to the next educator; and not doing a messy activity because it requires a longer cleanup.

In center child care settings, time management is tighter because rooms are scheduled for various uses (for example, one group has to vacate a room in time for another group to use it). Cleanup must be planned accordingly.

> When planning a schedule, give priority to children's needs over the convenience of the educator.

F. PROVIDING POSITIVE REINFORCEMENT

A constructive comment ("Congratulations to those who are putting the play things away quickly"), a smile, or an appreciative look is often all that is needed for children to understand that you approve of their behavior. There is no need to shower children with praise every time they perform their clean-up duties well. Reserve compliments for situations that really justify them, thus helping children to differentiate among the various degrees of achievement.

> Often, simply describing what the children are doing is enough to encourage them. "Stefan, I see that you can wash the paintbrushes very well." "Good, you are storing your boots in the right place." "It's fun to play on a clean table!"

If you observe children performing their tasks, you will be able to describe the behaviors in a personalized way. "Philip, you remembered how to put away the books on the display shelves! You really have a good memory!"

It is best to encourage children to surpass their own past performance, to beat their own record, instead of comparing them to their peers. "I bet you can tidy up faster than yesterday." "Jessie, I know you are capable of reading the labels on the shelves so that you can put the books back where they belong."

If a child shows a lack of interest, motivation, or attention, or has a problem with clumsiness, stay close to her and try to provide motivation. Ask the child to do something easy, as long as you ensure that the task is carried through. "There are two pieces missing in this puzzle. Look under the table to check if they might have fallen there." "Show me that you know how to place these blocks in the right container." "I put you in charge of cleaning up this section of the floor. Thanks!" "How can you put away the small cars so they can be easily found again?"

G. LETTING CHILDREN BEAR THE CONSEQUENCES

If a child makes a mess, such as spilling a glass of milk, playing with water in the bathroom, dropping playdough on the floor, or smearing paint on his face, do not scold him. Instead, require the child to participate in the cleanup. Learning through mistakes is more effective than verbal rebukes and the ensuing humiliation. Discipline in the context of democratic pedagogy focuses on straightening out mistakes rather than on punishment. The natural consequence of a behavior can be positive. For example, putting away a toy in the right place allows the child to find it easily and thus play with it longer.

H. BEING ACTIVE

By participating in the clean-up tasks yourself, you give children a concrete example that encourages them to follow in the same path. Moreover, by helping the child, you instill the idea of cooperation. "Do you want me to help you clean up the table?" Although children may be reticent to clean up when first asked, they will normally participate willingly after they observe adults taking concrete action. As a bonus, collaborative tidying up provides opportunities to speak with children about things that occurred during the previous activity—the fun they had, the conflicts they solved, or the sharing they participated in.

I. ENCOURAGING ONGOING TIDY-UP

In some cases, guiding children to pick up as they move from one activity to another is a good method to alleviate the chore of final tidy-up. In other cases, tidy-up time has to be left to the end, such as when children are taking turns finishing a puzzle. Assess each situation on its own merit, and help children negotiate the best solution among themselves. If a child must leave early, he may either tidy up early or check with the group to see if someone else wants to play with the same material. Obviously, the context and the child's age must be taken into account.

7.4 Tidy-up and clean-up games

After an activity, children often exhibit their need for a change by running around the room, fighting among themselves, or getting excited. This is the time to introduce cleanup by focusing on the pleasurable side of the activity. Merely repeating, "It's clean-up time. Come on, let's tidy up," is boring for children. After some time, they might not even hear the message. It becomes worn-out and ineffective. Using your imagination, you can think of strategies that encourage children to participate without goading. Indeed, using a variety of strategies through the year is a sound practice.

A. A JOB FOR EVERYONE

Assign a precise task to each child. "Javiera, please take care of the crayons." "Felix, please take the paper to the recycling bin." In certain cases, tasks can be randomly assigned. However, in most cases, tactfully matching a task to a child will overcome a child's negativity. Another efficient and fair method is to have everyone work on the same task. "Let's each pick up four pieces of paper and take them to the recycling bin."

B. THREE CHEERS FOR CREATIVITY!

Creating roles and imaginary characters is such fun! Why not become an astronaut who travels slowly through space carrying blocks to their box, or a delivery boy or girl who delivers crayons and paper to the shelves? Children can pretend to buy toys that must be put back in place. Observe the children's interests during play to find a gold mine of scripts that can be used to enliven clean-up time. Children pretending to be robots in the construction corner can be invited to continue their robot play at clean-up time. "The robots are now getting ready to carry the play materials back to their storage places."

Other ideas include wearing glasses like a scientist and using a pirate's telescope to look for things that need to be put away. A magician's glove may pick up toys or wash the table. Pretend to be a detective or a reporter who is fact-checking to see if everything is back in its place. Later, children can also act this part.

C. A BIT OF COMPLICITY

For the child, play cleanup is fun. Exploit this interest, and, with a little complicity, eliminate numerous verbal commands. By doing so you'll limit the disciplinary interventions that surface when you reach your limits. For example, encourage children in a direct way by proposing the following game: "I am closing my eyes. Tell me when you have finished putting away your toys, and I will count how many you placed on the shelf." Or, "I will clap my hands when you are through picking up the blocks."

D. DUSTING

In this game, using a wet cloth, the children dust a shelf prior to placing a toy on it. Very young children love to imitate adult actions, so they will be motivated to clean up. What better way to introduce them to clean-up tasks?

E. COUNTING

Here, children count aloud the number of toys picked up. Beginning at age three, children are usually interested in counting. "One toy, two toys, three toys. You are picking up a lot of toys, Kayne." Schoolagers like to learn words in a foreign language. They may enjoy learning to count in French, Spanish, Italian, and so forth. This is an opportunity for children from various ethnic groups to show their peers how to count in their native language.

F. MAGICAL VACUUM CLEANER

In this game, children pretend to vacuum the bits and pieces left after cutting out paper. The vacuum cleaner makes noise and eats up everything. Children love this kind of make-believe.

G. WHAT DO YOU WANT TO PUT AWAY?

By enticing children to make choices, they are happy to select what to put away, even within limited choices. "What do you want to put away, Leela?" "Miguel, do you want to take care of the puzzle or the crayons? You have the choice. You may decide what to do."

H. MUSIC TIME!

Why not enrich clean-up time with various types of music. Children generally like lively music and rhythms: reel, African music, rap, tango, waltz, military music, gospel, blues, and so forth. Invite children to clean up to the sound of the music (slow or fast). Ask them to freeze in place when the music stops, as in the game "statues" or "musical chairs." End the activity with slow, calming music to avoid overexciting the children.

I. PARALLEL PLAY FOR THE END OF CLEANUP

Children who are through with cleanup may engage in parallel play for a short time. Introduce games that are easy to start and to interrupt: guessing, miming, singing, or observation games are good choices. "Can you find yellow objects around the room?" "What do we call the season when leaves are falling down?" "Let's sing the song we learned this morning before the start of workshop."

J. A CHALLENGE FOR YOU

Give children small challenges. "Who can put away three objects?" "Who has arms capable of putting this truck back in place?" "Who can carry the mat very quietly?" No child will miss an opportunity to pick up the challenge and show off his abilities.

K. TIMING

Occasionally, use these techniques to encourage children to tidy up rapidly:

- Set an alarm to ring in five minutes.
- Use an hourglass placed where children can see the sand flow.
- Use a clock to observe the big hand reach the top position.
- Use a stopwatch for a super-fast clean-up game: "Five, four, three, two, one, let's go . . ."
- Play a familiar piece of music, and ask children to tidy up before the music ends.

Refrain from overusing these games to avoid generating excessive stress in children.

L. RELAY CLEANUP

Have children line up and pass materials from one child to the next up the line to the appropriate storage space, like an assembly line in a factory.

M. ONE DEMONSTRATION EQUALS A THOUSAND EXPLANATIONS

Tap a child's abilities by having her show the group how to properly put away materials. Children are often quite interested when a peer is the leader.

N. SPEAKING TOYS

Animate the toys by saying they are happy to be back in place. "Thanks, Jessica, for taking me back here. I can rest better when you put me back in my place." "I am happy to be on display," says the artwork, as Aren hangs it on the clothesline.

O. WAYS TO MOVE AROUND

Ask children to choose an original way to move around while putting away toys: hopping on one foot, marching like a penguin, or holding an object with only one hand. Suggest ideas and vary the game from one time to the next.

P. "SIMON SAYS"

This is a classic game. In this instance, "Simon says" motivates children to clean up. They must wait until the leader says "Simon says" and states the task to perform. "Simon says put the paper back in the container."

7.5 Clean-up songs

Nothing equals songs and nursery rhymes for announcing clean-up time, or singing along during cleanup. Children generally like this, even if they do not join in the singing.

Cleanup
(Tune: "Twinkle, Twinkle, Little Star")

> *It is time to clean up now.*
>
> *Clean up, clean up, we know how.*
>
> *We can clean up, you will see,*
>
> *Just how clean our room will be.*

Time to put toys away
(Tune: "Mary Had a Little Lamb")

> *Time to put the toys away,*
>
> *Toys away, toys away.*
>
> *Time to put the toys away,*
>
> *So we can have our snack* [or another action].

Tidy-up
(Tune: "Mary Had a Little Lamb")

> *Now it's time to tidy up,*
>
> *Tidy up, tidy up.*
>
> *Now it's time to tidy up*
>
> *And put our toys away.*

8

Group and Circle Time

CHAPTER CONTENTS

8.1 Grouping children

8.2 Encouraging children to participate

8.3 Encouraging children to get into a group

8.4 Where to group children

In an educational setting, many important elements are combined to turn the day into a successful experience for children and staff alike—schedule, room organization, educational programs, quality intervention, organization of routine activities, and so forth. At times, children are required to come together in large groups. Sometimes, large groups are formed by bringing together children from two rooms.

8.1 Grouping children

Suitable circle or group activities include discussing the preceding activity, planning the next one, distributing tasks, explaining directions or reminding children of them, sharing past experiences, singing, dancing, acting out a story, playing cooperation games, and relaxing. Generally, group time is short and can be divided into four stages: the beginning or trigger, the heart of the activity, the end and tidy-up time, and the transition to the next activity.

The gathering of children at the beginning of group or circle time must be simple and pleasant. Proponents of a democratic approach favor children being mostly active rather than passive, so circle time serves to reinforce the feeling of belonging to the group and helps new children to integrate. It can be helpful to use a song such as, "Hello, hello. . . . How are you? . . . It's good to see you. . . . How are you today?"

Starting circle without waiting for all children usually succeeds in bringing the rest of the children to circle. It is best to start distributing material and discussing the topic as soon as children begin forming a group. A verbal reminder may be enough to get all children into the circle. "Come, Morgan, there is a place just for you within the circle." However, some children prefer to observe circle from a distance (while they finish snack, for example). Judge each case individually, taking into account the situation and the child's age. Sometimes it is better to let children join circle at their own pace, letting them first finish what they are doing. "It makes sense to start the activity even if children are not finished with the one before it" (Hohmann and Weikart 1995, 289).

Preparation for circle should be done beforehand—gathering together CDs, materials, books, and so forth. If material has to be distributed, it should be done right at the beginning of circle time. Otherwise, children might start to disperse.

Closing of circle should also be well planned. Modify the last circle activity to act as a transition. "We will sing the last song, and then we will go to the changing area to get dressed!" Then, improvise the last song to introduce the next activity. "I am going to the changing area. I am getting dressed today. . . ."

8.2 Encouraging children to participate

The secret of a successful circle is flexibility and the ability to incorporate children's spontaneous suggestions. For example, Fatima is playing with her Velcro shoe fastener while sitting on the floor, and several children start to imitate her. Instead of trying to stop children from making this disturbing noise, apply a democratic approach to use this situation to explore for a little while what sounds children can make with their shoes: soft sounds, rubbing, scratching, and so forth. Children can be motivated by this activity, and their attention will be focused. After a short while, they probably will be more than ready to hear the story you wanted to read to them in the first place.

8.3 Encouraging children to get into a group

There are several ways to encourage children to meet at a specific place. Use sounds produced by an interesting instrument (flute, triangle) or sounds produced by the mouth (a different voice tone, interesting call-and-response themes—"hee-ha" by the educator, "ha-hee" echoed by the children—a rhyme, or a password to gain access to circle). Visual signals can also be used, including an arm above the head, a puppet, and so forth. You could begin a story: "Once upon a time, some children came from far away to sit beside me. They wanted to hear a story. They had just finished putting away their toys. There were one, two, three, four . . . children sitting next to me."

There are many different strategies to make circle a successful experience. Among others: tell a short story, hum a favorite tune, mime various things, play a guessing game involving sounds, or make a special drawing with a magical pen. Ideally, you should be at the same level as the children, while taking care not to damage your back. A variety of short activities will prevent children from getting bored. You may use a funny song to rekindle their interest. For example:

Magic Finger
(Tune: "Brother John")

Magic finger, magic finger

On your mouth, on your mouth

Put the magic finger, put the magic finger

On your mouth, on your mouth

8.4 **Where to group children**

The space for circle time should be large enough for children to sit or move comfortably. Some activities are better implemented around a table, others sitting around a carpet on the floor. Psychomotor games require a large open space where children can move easily. During summer, circle can be held outside in the shade of a tree. However, if a high level of concentration is required, it is better to group children away from distractions such as passersby, traffic, and birds.

Circle space must be clearly marked on the ground, and a specific sign or image for each child will help children find their particular spot. Consider using the same symbols as those used to identify the children's cubbie and mat (see Figure 8.1 on the next page). As with everything else, avoid rigidity, and use your imagination. In a democratic approach, children should be encouraged to solve disputes regarding their choice of place: taking turns sitting next to the educator, sitting close to a friend if certain conditions are met, and so forth.

FIGURE 8.1 **Group sitting arrangement for circle time, with pictures affixed on the floor**

9

Group Movements

C H A P T E R   C O N T E N T S

9.1 Strategies to avoid waiting times

9.2 Reducing large group movements

9.3 Ensuring children's safety

9.4 Little games

Getting to the changing area, the park, or the bathroom; walking to the gymnasium; going upstairs or downstairs or to another play space: these are all necessary group movements in early childhood settings. Unfortunately, these transition activities are often thought of as merely necessary evils to be expedited to get to the main activity. The constraints can be numerous: traffic jams, inadequate space, rigid schedule, fatigue, inappropriate organization, and so forth.

It is important to stop and think about these organizational issues in order to render group movement more effective and pleasant. This chapter covers such issues.

9.1 Strategies to avoid waiting times

Some group movements require a long wait for children and a lot of effort from the educator. You have to try to keep children in a line. You have to repeat directions several times and solve many guidance problems. The high level of noise and the proximity of other children require constant reminders to calm down. Short distances in small groups are preferable.

When more than one group is involved, educators can share tasks to facilitate the move. For example, when taking children outside to play, one educator can supervise the activities in the changing area while others take small groups of children outside as they are ready. Children can go

to the bathroom at the other end of the hallway with one educator, while another educator stays in the room.

Ideally, each room should have a door leading directly to the yard, but in reality this is rarely found. In fact, the setup of some educational centers complicates group movement. The yard and the bathroom are often far from the room.

It is always better to tell children a few minutes in advance where their group will go next. "After we finish washing our hands, we will go to the snack room."

9.2 Reducing large group movements

To reduce the frequency of group movements, consider giving more autonomy to older children. They can be given the responsibility to go to the bathroom on their own. Children must clearly understand the rules pertaining to such tasks: for example, only one child at a time goes to the bathroom; the educator must be informed beforehand; no "hanging out" is allowed; and so forth.

9.3 Ensuring children's safety

Be particularly vigilant when younger children go up and down stairs. While keeping an eye on the whole group, show the younger ones how to hold on to the banister, how to stay in a single file at a safe distance, and how to look ahead. Decide whether to walk ahead or behind children to ensure the best supervision possible.

It might not always be possible to prevent children from running when they are in a hurry to go outside, but high-speed traffic, whether indoors or out, is a recipe for collisions and falls. There are several ways to control this situation: Ask older children to slow down the group and to share the duties of group control with adults. Play games that encourage the children to move slowly. Teach children to be careful and to solve problems. Show children how to keep to the right in traffic and not to run up and down stairs. There should be a clear system of rules on group movement that are to be followed by everyone at the center.

Outings to the park or to a surrounding area may be pleasant and relaxing for children. However, for safety reasons, there should always be two adults involved. If you must go out alone with a group of children, bring a cell phone with you in case of emergency. Note that this will be insufficient if you yourself are the victim of serious injury or sudden illness. Plan well in advance so you are not placed in an unfortunate situation.

All educators need to know where the first-aid kit is and should have easy access to it, without making it accessible to children. A first-aid kit should be taken along when outside the center, including to the playground. Verify the first-aid-kit contents regularly. Remember that it has to include gloves to prevent exposure to blood or other bodily secretions. Also, always keep a pair of gloves in your pocket when going out.

9.4 Little games

Here again, little games can facilitate group movements. See the suggestions in Box 9.1.

BOX 9.1 **Ideas to get moving**

- Move one behind another in various ways: as a train, two by two, and so forth. Take on an imaginary role as a whole group or as individuals: a giant centipede, a caterpillar, a robot, and so forth.

- Walk in an unusual way: on tiptoes, on heels, with arms crossed on chest, as a cat looking for prey. On rainy or very cold days, when it is impossible to go out, walking through the center in a funny way can give children a bit of exercise. Another option: attach small bells to chenille craft stems and tie them around the children's ankles. Ask children to move without making noise. When the children arrive at their destination, they can make their bells ring by dancing to music. Choose ways to move according to the children's level of development.

- More walking games: Walk pretending to carry a sleeping baby in your arms. Walk like a mouse. Walk with "magic" shoes on that do not make noise. Walk like a secret agent.

- Chose a queen or a king at the head or the tail of the line. The other children can be princes and princesses. Use a rhyme to choose the queen or the king (or other roles).

- Have children carry playthings along with them. They enjoy being helpful.

- When there is a problem, enforce the rule that when a child leaves his place, he loses it.

- To rapidly form a line, make each child pick a number or a letter out of a box or bag.

- To slow down the walking, have children touch the walls whenever possible.

- Play traffic lights: Red is stop. Green, walk normally. Yellow, walk slowly.

- When you arrive at your destination, use a password or gesture for each child to be authorized to leave the line.

- All children hold on to an extended spring toy (for example, a Slinky) so that they stay together.

Group movements outside of the center call for additional safety measures: strict supervision by at least two adults, a complete and up-to-date first-aid kit, an EpiPen autoinjector for children with allergies, safe transport that respects all laws, and telephone numbers of parents. All outings require thorough preparation in close collaboration with members of the center administration as well as with parents.

10

Arrival and Departure

CHAPTER CONTENTS

10.1 A warm and personal welcome

10.2 Saying hello with a smile

10.3 Calling children by their first names

10.4 Staff stability

10.5 Helping children and parents separate at
the beginning of the day

10.6 Taking attendance

10.7 Helping children and parents leave

10.8 Dealing with parents who are late for pickup

10.9 Little games

We are all influenced in one way or another by the first moments we spend with a person or group. Young children are particularly sensitive to gesture and tone of voice, to the words and attitudes of the people who welcome them.

Arrival and departure are destabilizing transition activities if children have to change educators, go from one place to another, or adapt to a different set of rules or to other children, possibly of different ages, and so forth. In child care centers, children usually arrive early in the morning and leave at the end of the afternoon. In preschools, there might be two arrivals (in the morning and in the early afternoon) and two departures (at the end of the morning and at the end of the afternoon). Who would be able to remain physically and emotionally stable while having to adapt to so many different people and environments in such a short time?

Stressed by their work, with supper to prepare and all sorts of responsibilities—including requests from educators—parents may fail to focus on their children as they rush to drop them off at the center or to pick them up. In an era when everyone is in a hurry, the need to slow down when taking one's child to the center is not always evident. Parents all have valid reasons to explain their rush. "I do not have time." "I am in a hurry." "I am going to be late." "My boss is expecting me." "My day is not finished." "I have lots to do at home." "I am buried in work." Child care centers are torn between ensuring the well-being of the child and yielding to the pressure sometimes created by parents. However, it is important that both center staff and parents take the time to make the transitions of arrival and departure positive times for children.

10.1 A warm and personal welcome

The way children are welcomed in a child care center is crucial. The type of welcome received can make or break the day for a child: welcoming children with a friendly smile or, alternatively, harboring a forced smile; speaking friendly words such as, "How is our Bruno today?" or, alternatively, being in a bad mood and showing it; looking indiffer-

ent or, alternatively, looking interested. These are all behaviors observed in child care settings. Children should be greeted properly, regardless of your mood. To ensure children's well-being, you must display a professional and friendly attitude. Be consistent and available at all times. When welcoming children, smile and speak to them in a friendly voice. Greet them by their first name and show pleasure in seeing them.

It is important for children to be able to make choices right away upon arrival: finding something interesting to play with, observing other children, speaking with friends or with an educator, or finishing something started the day before. Time spent in front of the television must be kept to a strict minimum. This also includes watching videos, since children do this a lot at home.

Welcoming the parent who brings the child is a mark of respect for the child as well as for the parent (Martin, Poulin, and Falardeau 1992). Child care centers should be a welcoming place for parents. You are responsible for thanking the parent for their cooperation (for example, for bringing a second set of clothes when asked, for providing follow-up comments about their child's behavior, or for describing what the child does at home). You will often have to ask for information about the child's condition. "How was his night? Is he feeling better today?" Occasionally, a meeting or a telephone conversation will have to be planned to discuss a particular problem in-depth. At the end of a tiring day, in the presence of other parents and children, is not the time for a fruitful exchange.

Unfortunately, it is often very difficult to have regular exchanges with parents when they are forced to drop off and pick up their children in the hallway, without being able to go into the room where children spend a big part of their day. In some centers, children are even sent to the parent via an intercom system, thus preventing any communication between parents and educators. A walkie-talkie is seen by many as a way of preventing parents from circulating in the center and of speeding up departure. This does not meet children's needs, and it should be banned in centers practicing democratic pedagogy. However, a cell phone may be useful when children are away from the center. Do not forget to have a list posted at the entrance of the center that tells parents where to pick up their child. Indicate clearly the name of the group, the day of the week, the hour, and the activity.

Conducting arrival and departure transitions with an emphasis on minimizing the loss of time and maximizing efficiency has no place in a center that focuses on respect and dignity for children and parents. To work for the child, you will need to invest time and energy in establishing a positive relationship with parents, even if it seems difficult to do so with some parents. You'll need preparation and determination to reach a timid, uninterested, or perhaps unpleasant parent. Perseverance, conviction, and consistency are indispensable qualities if you are to build a constructive relationship with parents who are difficult to approach. Above all, do not wait until there is a problem with the child to start speaking with the parent. The sense of partnership that is essential to children's well-being is slowly built up over time.

Occasionally, because of a desire to reassure parents that their child is well cared for at the center, educators take too dominant a role vis-à-vis the child in the presence of a parent. Such behavior may make parents jealous or uneasy, and it should be avoided. Educators must recognize the primary role of parents toward their children and avoid competing with them.

Ideally, educators, parents, and children should adopt a three-way system of communication (Martin, Poulin, and Falardeau 1992, 86). Arrival and departure transitions constitute ideal conditions for this communication. For example, when a parent and an educator discuss a child, the child should be included in the conversation. This shows respect for the child. "Max, I am telling your father that you have learned to solve conflicts well. Are you proud of yourself?" "Daleesha, your mommy and I are going to work together to teach you how to use the toilet. Do you think this is a good idea?" "Alex, did you tell your daddy that we started to plant a garden today? You can tell him about it during the trip home."

Educators need to respect privacy. Never talk with a parent about another child and never talk with a parent about another parent (Martin, Poulin, and Falardeau 1992). Moreover, professional ethics dictate that all staff keep information confidential—personal information is disclosed only to those who have the right and the need to know it.

The setting must be suitable for a positive arrival and departure transition. Have available a chair to take off boots and a space to put them (or shoe covers to enable parents to enter the center without making the floor dirty). Hang a welcome banner in several languages if the center is multiethnic. Put up a bulletin board specifically for parents—one that is attractive and not overloaded. It should include general information relevant to the center such as the time of the next outing; menus; an activity program; pamphlets and posters on health, safety, and education (the proper use of a car seat, the addresses of helpful organizations for families having various problems); some literature that parents can take with them; drawings and pictures of their children (periodically renewed); and so forth.

10.2 Saying hello with a smile

Smiling is a function unique to human beings. It is one of the first facial expressions decoded by infants, and is one to which they are very receptive. Socio-affective development is enhanced through contact with people who exhibit warm behavior. Smiles and friendly voices constitute important capital for children's emotional health. A seven-year-old who tells his educator that her smile brings sun into his day attests to that.

Remember that moving the seventeen muscles involved in smiling is a beneficial exercise that should be performed as often as possible when in front of children and parents!

10.3 Calling children by their first names

Educators should call children by the first names chosen by their parents, without transforming them or using diminutives. "Good morning, Sumiko." When you have questions about a name and its pronunciation, just ask a parent to ensure you pronounce the name well. It is important for a name not to become a subject of mockery or a cause of rejection by others. In such a situation, you need to communicate with a parent to find a satisfactory solution for the child. It is also best not to use affectionate names such as "sweetie" or "love" or to use plays on surnames such as "Speedy Martin" or "Pepper Mills."

10.4 Staff stability

It is reassuring for children arriving at the child care center to recognize familiar faces. Having a stable core of staff is essential. It is especially important for very young children, for children who are just starting at the center, for those who attend part-time, and for those who are not native English speakers. Ideally, the main educator should be present either upon the children's arrival or at their departure. Because she spends several hours a day with the children, she is the one best suited to exchange information with parents. It is also advisable for the coordinator or person responsible for the child care center to be present to meet with parents if they need information that falls within her area of responsibility: fees and payments, registration renewal, and so forth.

10.5 Helping children and parents separate at the beginning of the day

Leaving a loved one can be very difficult for young children. It is normal that they cry, cling to their parents, complain, or refuse to go to an educator. Separation anxiety is linked to many factors: previous (negative) experience, parental attitude, health of the child, a parent returning from a long absence, the child's disposition, the family situation, the presence of new staff, and so forth.

Although children can be vulnerable at any age, those ages eight months to three years are particularly sensitive to separation from their parents at the beginning of the day. Think about the attitude of two-year-olds regarding their self-assertion and their newfound ability to say "no," or about children who are just entering kindergarten without having any previous experience in a child care center. Fortunately, there are strategies to help children separate from their parents and become integrated into the group.

- Make available to them games and objects they like.
- Provide points of reference to give them a feeling of security. Tell them beforehand what they will be doing during the morning. Remind them of what happened the day before.
- Allow them to keep a security (transitional) object for a while.
- Implement a ritual with the parent upon arrival, such as the parent giving the child a hug and kiss, taking the child to the door of the room, and waving good-bye.

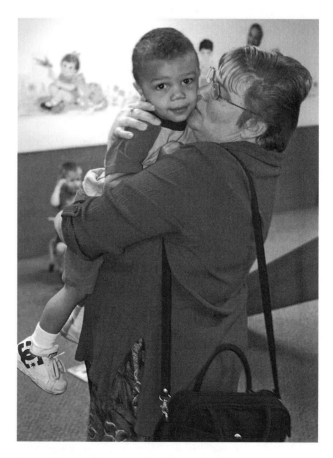

During the first weeks of adaptation to a child care center, children may react strongly to the departure of a parent. Many parents find these moments painful, especially if they do not know how to act. Some parents leave rapidly without saying good-bye to their child, while others linger too long, allowing the child to cling to them. Still others demand that their child stop crying, or they tell a lie such as, "I will come back in a little while." This negative behavior is often the manifestation of a certain sense of helplessness rather than a lack of sensitivity. With objectivity and perseverance, you can help the parent and child negotiate the necessary transition between home and child care center, and help each adapt well to this new situation.

While making sure you do not create excessive dependence (for instance, by continually holding the child in your arms or holding his hand), you should keep visual and verbal contact with a child who is affected by his parent's departure. It is important to recognize the feelings of pain, fear, and anger being experienced by the child. "I know you are angry that daddy left because you would have loved staying with him." "I see that it is difficult for you to get used to so many things occurring at the same time. I am here to help you and protect you until your parents come to pick you up." You may help the child to progressively relax and get interested in her surroundings by showing her play materials and playing with her. Children need about three to six weeks to adapt to the child care center. Regular attendance, positive parenting, and educator attitudes facilitate the child's adaptation to the child care center.

10.6 Taking attendance

As required by law, you must keep an attendance sheet for each child. The director or manager of the child care center has the duty to update the attendance record every day.

Generally, attendance is taken upon the children's arrival. It can also be taken two or three more times a day, depending on the child care center. Dates, days, and hours of attendance, both projected and actual, must be indicated in writing. Attach a pencil to the attendance book to avoid wasting time trying to find one. Some tricks may also be used as shortcuts: For older children, stamp the space or draw a smiley face next to their name on the list.

10.7 Helping children and parents leave

To facilitate children's departure, their personal belongings must be ready. When applicable, give any information sheet directly to parents. When parents are personally handed documents, they naturally feel more concerned and are less inclined to let the documents remain at the bottom of their child's backpack. Moreover, this offers an opportunity to communicate with parents who are not very talkative.

Departure, as well as arrival, requires consistency in its ritual. Do not pressure children, but gently guide them to tidy up and get ready to go home. The ritual could include a hug and saying good-bye. It is important to anticipate the difficulty some children have in interrupting play, even with their parent asking them to get ready. One child may be in the middle of a conversation with another child, while still another is desperately looking for a lost object. There might also be problems if a particular parent speaks with you for a long time about random matters, monopolizing your attention and preventing you from working. Fortunately, there are techniques for dealing with such situations. See Box 10.1.

BOX 10.1 **Techniques to help with difficult departures**

- Clarify the roles of child, parent, and educator. For example, make sure parents begin taking care of their children as soon as they enter the child care center.

- Politely excuse yourself when a parent keeps talking and return to your tasks. "I am sorry I can't talk longer with you. I need to go back to the children."

- Make departure coincide with outdoor play. This way, children will already be dressed and ready to leave when their parents arrive.

- In a subtle way, guide the child (and the parent) to the changing area, while reminding him to take home his drawings, which have been placed in his cubbie.

- Have a conversation about what the child will do at home, and encourage her to leave. Remind her of when she will come back to the center. "Have a good evening, Brynn. See you tomorrow."

- Remind the child of one event that occurred during the day, and encourage him to tell his parent about it on the way home.

- Implement a departure ritual where parents first have to read their child's journal in the changing area before entering the main room. This will make your verbal exchange more productive and more on topic. It also allows you to check whether the written information has been understood.

- With a slow child or with a very talkative one, use a timer that warns the child after five minutes that it is time to go.

In cases when you have to help a parent who has to leave rapidly with the child (supper, activity), it is important to make it clear that this is an exceptional situation and not a procedure that is to be repeated on a regular basis. If, however, it is to be a daily occurrence, a written agreement with the parent should be put into effect, noting the irregularity of the procedure and the reasons for it.

10.8 Dealing with parents who are late for pickup

When parents arrive after closing, the center must have measures in place to counter abuses and limit discussions. Consider a fine for lateness. It is important to enforce these measures consistently. They can be spelled out in the introductory document given to parents when they register their child. A sign on the parents' bulletin board can also refresh their memories.

The feelings of the child who is left alone after everybody has left must also be taken into account. Reassure her, continue watching her, and explain what is happening.

10.9 Little games

A positive environment will help everyone get through the arrival and departure transition in a relaxed way. Here again, games come to the rescue.

- Upon a child's arrival, show her a feeling chart and ask her to point to the picture that best describes her mood.

- Preschool children can be welcomed in a foreign language: *bonjour* (French), *bon giorno* (Italian), *buenos dias* (Spanish), *kaliméra* (Greek), *guten Morgen* (German), and so forth.

- Invent a special way to say good morning, perhaps including a particular physical movement. (Five-year-olds and up.)

11

Unavoidable Waiting

CHAPTER CONTENTS

11.1 Countering unavoidable waits

11.2 Organizing unavoidable waits

11.3 Making the best of the situation

    A. Verbal games

    B. Visual observation games

    C. Listening games

    D. Hand-eye coordination games

    E. Symbolic games/role play

    F. Audiovisual games

    G. Fine-motor games

    H. Gross-motor games

    I. Breathing games (three-year-olds)

    J. Olfactory games (two-year-olds)

    K. Tactile games

    L. Vocal games

    M. Artistic games

    N. Self-massage (two-year-olds)

Early childhood education programs that practice democratic pedagogy approach waiting in the same way as the other activities of the day. That is to say, these transitions can be turned into harmonious situations in which the children can participate and not become tired, impatient, or annoyed. This happens by paying attention to time management and the environment in partnership with the other members of the educational team. Unfortunately, there are educational settings where children are subjected to long waits several times a day in large groups—they are sometimes required to stand, in silence, without much movement and, above all, without disruption (for example, four-years-olds expected to wait calmly in line to go to the toilet or to brush their teeth). This generates tension in the group. The proper approach will diminish this tension. It is always difficult to change well-anchored habits, but such an approach is well worth the effort.

11.1 Countering unavoidable waits

"It is essential that children learn to wait at a young age." This remark is often repeated by those who take care of children, preoccupied as they are with initiating them into the harsh realities of life. Indeed, it is normal to have to wait even when one is small, but it is important to keep in mind that the time perception of children is very different from that of adults. Frequent waiting that is prolonged and disproportionate to the stage of development may be harmful to children's sense of confidence and security. In any case, social, family, and school environments give rise to numerous delays in the lives of children. In the company of close relatives, children have many occasions to exercise patience over the course of a day: during car trips; waiting in the check-out line at a grocery store, at a doctor's office, or in a restaurant; waiting for meals to be prepared or while mom talks on the telephone; and so forth.

Waiting in a small group during a familiar event such as a family activity does not require the same control on the part of the child as waiting in a large, impersonal group in an educational setting. Furthermore, waiting for two minutes is

not at all the same thing for a two-year-old as for an eight-year-old. Such a wait may seem interminable, especially for a toddler or for someone in the midst of a tantrum. A four-year-old once asked an educator about a five-minute wait: "Is it a child's five minutes or an adult's five minutes?" Time perception inevitably involves a subjective dimension (Lauzon 1990). Children may comment, "It's too long" or alternatively, "It was very quick" or "I can't wait anymore." Such a subjective appreciation of time is true for adults as well. Bear in mind the limitations of children when it comes to their capacity to wait. Keep waiting to a minimum, since the longer the wait, the more damage done to the development of activities and to the dynamics of the group. But remember, "Waiting time can be reduced but it cannot always be eliminated" (Hohmann and Weikart 1995, 289).

Children must be able to move—to use their motor capacities, to expend their energy omnipresent in the lower age groups—without being obliged to wait for an educator to complete a static task like taking attendance or to wait silently in a row while other children finish an activity before going outside to play. The desire of children to move has nothing to do with hyperactivity. It is normal and, most of the time, indicative of good health. "Long periods of waiting encourage children to behave inappropriately. This is not because children wish to misbehave. It is merely their natural desire to keep busy" (Davidson 1982, 196).

If, as a regular occurrence, eight, ten, or twenty children have to wait in line to wash their hands, or wait in the changing area wearing heavy snowsuits before going outside to play or wait to get an educator's help while she talks in the corridor with a colleague, and if these situations are repeated and prolonged, a serious analysis of the planning, organization, and educational methodology is needed to correct the situation. However, it is not catastrophic if, in spite of good organization, children still have to wait on occasion. Waiting to eat because the caterer is late and waiting during a trip because an accident has occurred are unavoidable incidents that need not generate trouble. In these situations it is important not to tire the children. To prevent total disorganization when unforeseen situations occur, have children sit in a line along a wall, on the floor, on chairs, or on a bench, maintaining, if possible, a minimal distance between each child.

Knowing how to adapt is a necessary strength when events conspire to produce unforeseen situations. In this sense, your attitude as the educator plays a determining role in the quality and pedagogical value of waiting activities. "Consider all the tasks that must be accomplished in a given time frame and allow enough time so that routine tasks can be handled in a relaxed, unhurried way" (Brickman and Taylor 1991, 137).

11.2 Organizing unavoidable waits

In democratic pedagogy, waiting usually refers to unavoidable waits, when delays are reduced to a minimum both in number and in duration. Waiting for the bus before leaving on an educational trip, waiting for another group to join in a visit to a local pastry shop, waiting for the arrival of a surprise guest—these are common occurrences, and there is nothing dramatic about them. Such experiences can even be positive if the delay remains reasonable and you are able to find an effective method to occupy the children. Take advantage of a song recently learned, do a little physical exercise proposed by a child, or ask a child to tell some riddles. There are many such methods that enhance unavoidable waits.

To diminish the number and duration of delays, children should have the benefit of an environment organized to allow them to act as individuals with a degree of autonomy. Here are some examples:

- Give children the freedom to go to the toilet on their own. This can be done if toilets are close to the classroom.
- If the toilets are located farther away, such as at the end of the hall, have one educator stay with the group of children who are going to the bathroom while another educator stays in the room with the remaining children.
- Make afternoon snack an individual choice. Children may choose whether to come to the snack table to take their snack. This eliminates having to wait in an orderly manner

while others are finishing snack before going on to another activity.

- Allow children to play quietly after waking up from a nap, without having to wait until everyone else is awake.

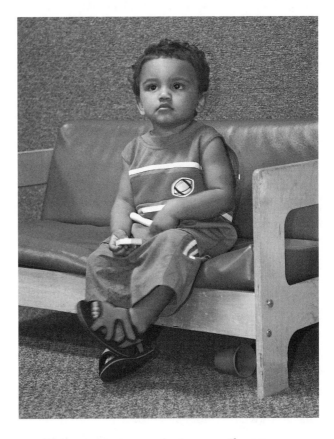

These strategies can be just as effective as actually finding ways to avoid delays. The reduction of the duration and frequency of waiting times depends in great measure on the participation of the children themselves. It is your responsibility to encourage this in accordance with their stage of development.

According to the principles of democratic pedagogy, the rare moments of waiting in educational centers must be dynamic. Children must be able to communicate, to express their own thoughts, and to discover and act within their environment. They must be able to talk with each other, to help each other tidy up when they are finished playing, to put their own dishes away, to help dress the youngest children, to go to the toilet when they feel like it (and not just because it is the time designated for that activity), to leave the changing area under the supervision of an educator when they are dressed, and so forth. They must be able to make choices with educators rather than just responding to commands.

Strategies intended to diminish the disruption caused by occasional delays must not be based only on verbal methods of control. Too often children hear, "Stop talking," "Stay in your chair," "I will help each of you in turn," "I only have two hands," "Wait your turn to wash your hands," "There is only one sink," "That's three times I've asked you not to move forward," "Be patient, children, I will finish arranging the cots soon. I am just about to take out play materials," and so forth. Most of the time, verbal instructions are not understood by children. Furthermore, educators who try to maintain absolute control over a group of children—who try to do everything in their way and according to their rhythm—place children in a state of dependence harmful to children's development and put children into situations likely to create tension in the flow of daily activities.

While children wait for their educator to finish gathering up art materials, to serve snack, or to arrange the workshop accessories that were scattered all over the floor, they tend to busy themselves, following their own interests. It's times like these—when children are forced to wait—that they become distracted and trouble starts. They play with what is close at hand, which often means their peers. They talk, play with their hands, and try to calm younger children, who may be wiggling around. After a minute or two, patience and imagination reach their limit, and trouble starts: tears, rushing about, teasing, hitting, and so forth. The educator must then use disciplinary measures to bring the children back to order, while at the same time attempting to finish her task. The educator's frustration, the efforts taken to reestablish control, and the children's fatigue undermine the atmosphere of the group. Then, discouraged, the educator wonders why the children are being so difficult. "Constant misbehavior at these times brings teacher disapproval, contributing to a child's negative self-esteem, a poor child/teacher relationship, and an uncomfortable classroom atmosphere" (Davidson 1982, 196). See Table 11.1 for examples of situations to encourage and to avoid.

11.3 Making the best of the situation

Educators need a variety of methods at the ready to make unavoidable waits more agreeable. These are often the little "extras" that make the difference between tiresome waits and bearable ones. For example, movement through the corridors often takes place in large groups, generating delays. Why not decorate the walls with attractive posters, photos, or drawings made by the children to occupy their attention at these moments?

To limit the disinterest and boredom of the children during transitions, a little imagination and preparation will suffice. Don't forget that moments of waiting may constitute ideal occasions for creating calm and getting the attention of the children. You'll benefit by evaluating which strategies best achieve this for your group. "Transitions between different parts of the routine are a good opportunity for movement experiences" (Brickman and Taylor 1991, 108).

Numerous books and Web sites examine ideas on this subject. The activities proposed here are compatible with democratic pedagogy: creativity, pleasure, learning from games, cooperation. At all times, try to take into consideration the reactions and suggestions of the children and integrate them into the course of activities. "Remember that children do not like to sit and keep quiet" (Hohmann and Weikart 1995, 289). It is a good idea to keep a supply of materials on hand to avoid frustration and unavoidable waits. Materials for the waiting games suggested here should be gathered into attractive, easy-to-handle boxes in order to be effective. All age guidelines are approximate.

A. VERBAL GAMES

- Think of names of animals living in the air, on the ground, and in water. (Four-year-olds.) Variation: name animals that live on a farm, in a zoo, at home.
- Learn to say a small series of numbers in English, French, Spanish, Italian, or a native language of children in your setting. (Four-year-olds.)
  One–two–three–four–five–Yay! (English)
  Un–deux–trois–quatre–cinq–Yé! (French)
  Uno–dos–tres–cuatro–cinco–Bravo! (Spanish)

Uno–dué–tré–quattro–cinqué–Bravissimo! (Italian)

- Find rhymes. An educator or game leader says, "What should I put on my hat?" A player must find a rhyming answer. "On my hat, I put my cat." Variations: "What will glow on my hat?" "What do I need in my backpack?" (Three-year-olds.)
- Listen to known rhymes and songs. (Two-year-olds.)
- Play guessing games, riddles, word puzzles, and charades tailored to the children's capacities. Keep a bank of these word games, and update it regularly. (Three-year-olds.)

TABLE 11.1 **Waiting situations to encourage and to avoid**

Encourage these situations	Avoid these situations
Children rarely wait.	Children often wait.
Children wait for a short time.	Children wait for a long time.
Children do not wait in line.	Children wait in line.
Children are allowed to be active and speak with a low voice.	Children have to stay still and be silent.
Activities end progressively, and the next activity begins in small groups.	Activities stop at once, and children are all grouped together.
Only a few children gather simultaneously at the same place.	Many children gather simultaneously at the same place.
Two educators work as a team and share work.	A single educator performs all the work alone.
Educator focuses on only three to five directions at once.	Educator presents several directions at once.
Educator accepts that the outcome is not perfect while keeping control of the group.	Educator seeks perfection at all cost and may lose control of the group.
Educator uses a variety of guidance strategies.	Educator always uses the same guidance strategies.
Educator does not limit herself to verbal directions—she also uses sounds and visual signals.	Educator uses mainly verbal directions.
In difficult situations, educator remains calm and composed while being firm and convincing.	In difficult situations, educator screams at children, threatens them, and so forth.
Educator makes decisions in collaboration with children.	Educator decides for the children.
Educator gives responsibilities to children.	Educator performs all tasks herself.
Educator gives responsibilities to children according to their capacities.	Educator gives to children responsibilities that are either too difficult or too easy to do.
Educator reflects upon her guidance techniques and adjusts them if needed.	Educator always uses the same guidance techniques (by habit or by reflex) without trying to understand what is happening.

- Give a single answer to many different questions: For example, sausages: "What are you doing on weekends?"—"Sausages." "What do you see when you look at yourself in the mirror?"—"Sausages." "What do you take along to the museum?"—"Sausages." And so on. (Five-year-olds.) Variation: Make the game more complicated by asking children not to laugh. Use another word for the answer.

- Invent the beginning of a story, and let children develop it. "Let's open the big book of our imagination. That morning, while the baby foxes were still sleeping . . ." or "A big red ball was dreaming of making a trip . . ." (Three-year-olds.) Variation: Stimulate children to figure out what comes next in a story by having them pick out a picture from a stack: animals, objects, and so forth. (Five-year-olds.)

B. VISUAL OBSERVATION GAMES

- Suggest an observation game. "What am I wearing that is shiny?" "Name something in the room that is blue." "Name the smallest object here." "Who within the group has brown eyes?" (Three-year-olds.)

- Show children a large illustration (landscape, animal, food), and then ask them to picture it in their heads. Ask them to look at the picture in their heads and try to observe its colors, shapes, and textures. This can be done without talking. (Five-year-olds.)

- Ask a child to hide where he can't see or hear what's going on. This player will take on the role of a scientist who has invented robots that suddenly become very undisciplined. They decide to follow their own leader. The other children—the robots—form a circle, sitting on the floor. Select a robot leader among the children. When the leader makes a gesture, all the robots must imitate her. The "scientist" comes back, stands in the middle of the circle, and tries to identify the leader. (Five-year-olds.)

- The game leader throws into the air a light scarf, a thin leaf, a small piece of cellophane, a sheet of paper, or a feather. While the object is in the air, the children perform a required action (scratching their nose, clicking their tongue, humming). As soon as the object hits the ground, the children stop the action. Variation: Stay very still and listen to the sound made by the object falling on the ground. (Two-year-olds.)

- Place familiar objects on a table (in the beginning, three objects will suffice). Ask children to observe them. Cover the objects with a cloth and ask the children to name them. Ask some questions: "What objects do we use to . . . ?" "What object is blue?" (Two-year-olds.) Variation: Remove an object, and then ask the children to identify the missing object.

- Have children imitate gestures made by an educator as if they were in front of a mirror. (Two-year-olds.)

- Look at books. Change them regularly.

- Use a visual signal, such as a special crazy glove, to get the children's attention. It could also be a funny poster, a flag, or colored cards, each with a special meaning. (Two-year-olds.)

C. LISTENING GAMES

- With eyes closed, children try to guess what object has fallen on the ground: pencil, ball, spoon, paper plate, and so forth.

- Follow coded directions to move a hand as instructed by an educator: *Quilibi* means point the index finger. *Watawa* means make a fist. *Gurubu* means turn the palm of the hand toward the ground. *Mogogo* means turn the palm of the hand upward. (Five-year-olds.)

- Guess the name of songs hummed by an educator or a child. Variation: A child can articulate the words in silence, and the group guesses by reading lips. (Two-year-olds.)

- Guess sounds heard in the surrounding environment. "What sounds are coming from the next room?" Variation: Identify recorded sounds. (Two-year-olds.)

- Fill small empty plastic containers with various substances: rice, sand, paper pellets. Have children identify the contents of the container from the sounds made. (Three-year-olds.)

- Ask children to imitate various simple rhythms you make with your body: loud or soft claps, a finger hitting a palm, clapping with two hands, and so forth. (Four-year-olds.)
- Tell a familiar story such as "Three Little Pigs" or "Snow White," but introduce some errors into the story. Children must try to identify the errors. (Five-year-olds.)
- With eyes closed, children point to the educator, who moves around while she speaks. (Five-year-olds.)
- "Do what I say, and not what I do." A child names an action while performing another. For example, he asks the others to brush their hair while he brushes his teeth. Children must do what is asked and not what is observed. (Five-year-olds.)

D. HAND-EYE COORDINATION GAMES

- Give each child a sturdy transparent plastic bottle filled with water and a few drops of food coloring. The bottles must be watertight. Invite children to shake them and observe what happens in the bottles. (Two-year-olds.)
- Leaf through children's books or homemade albums containing personal drawings, pictures of the group taken at different times, interesting cuttings from magazines, and so forth. Purchase photo albums with plastic pockets to protect the pictures. You can group the pictures according to themes, such as food, animals, people of different ethnic groups, transportation, feelings, landscapes, pictures taken during field trips, and so forth. Older children can help make theme albums. Such albums can also be used to illustrate values such as kindness, health, and the joy of living. Have a camera ready at all times to capture events and to take pictures for the walls of the room and the photo albums.
- Remember that two- and three-year-olds do not easily share objects with peers. They much prefer manipulating an object of their own. For this reason, prepare little magic brown paper bags stuffed with pieces of an old puzzle, a plastic picture, a little mirror, a mitten to put on. (Two-year-olds.)

E. SYMBOLIC GAMES/ROLE PLAY

- Offer children theme kits, easily taken out and put away, containing safe and interesting material: small figures, puppets, plastic-coated pictures. (Three-year-olds.)
- Play with puppets (finger puppets, hand puppets, marionettes). (Two-year-olds.)
- Make associations from a simple object: cardboard cylinder, ball, scarf, sheet of paper. "What does it remind you of?" "What does it look like?" "What can you pretend it is?" For example, a ball can be a fruit, a cylinder can be a telescope, a sheet can be a plate, etc. Miming and role-playing can be added. This activity develops children's creativity and abstract thinking. (Five-year-olds.)
- Play at "sleeping," staying motionless, with eyes open as long as possible. Only eye blinking and breathing are allowed. By making faces, a magician tries to "wake up" these strange sleepers and make them move without touching them. (Five-year-olds.)
- Mime simple actions:
  - Through direct suggestion—stretch like a cat, move like a flower in the wind, rock a baby. (Two-year-olds.)
  - Through indirect suggestion—crawl like an animal, repeat a recent outdoor activity. (Three-year-olds.)

- Mime various feelings: joy, sadness, shyness, anger. (Four-year-olds.)
- Mime a daily action by making very small or very big gestures: brushing teeth, putting on a sweater, eating. (Four-year-olds.)
- Permit children to use acceptable physical outlets in well-supervised situations. Examples: hit a pillow; shout in the yard; play with cold, hard playdough; tear and throw paper; pop bubbles in bubble wrap; dance to lively music; mime a song. Children need your help to channel their aggressiveness and their energy. (Two-year-olds.)

F. AUDIOVISUAL GAMES

- Have children listen to familiar rhymes and songs while you show pictures associated with them. (Place a collection of pictures in a box or in a binder to facilitate this.) (Two-year-olds.)
- Invite children to imitate actions you perform while you describe what to do: "Hands on head." "Hands on shoulders." "Index finger on nose." Variation: Make "mistakes" between what you do and what you say, and let the children find the error. (Two-year-olds.)
- Read a picture book to the children. (Two-year-olds.)

G. FINE-MOTOR GAMES

- Ask children to put on gloves. (Three-year-olds.)
- Sew Velcro strips onto a glove, and organize a fishing game where children grab objects made of felt or fabric with the glove. (Two-year-olds.)
- Provide plastic containers with screw tops, or large bolts and screws to manipulate. (Three-year-olds.)
- Provide small photos or picture albums to manipulate. (Two-year-olds.)

H. GROSS-MOTOR GAMES

- Make a simple obstacle course. For example, walk on imaginary stones, or walk around furniture. The course can lead to a magic place, such as a castle represented by a large, decorated cardboard box or an upside-down table. (Three-year-olds.)
- Move from one place to another with a dry sponge on the head, trying to keep it from falling. (Four-year-olds.)
- Play "Simon Says": "Simon says place your hands on your head." (Children perform the action.) "Place your hands on your ears." (Children do nothing, unless "Simon says.") (Four-year-olds.)
- Mime action songs. Many folk songs work well with children: "Head, Shoulders, Knees, and Toes," "If You're Happy," "Miss Mary Mack," "Open, Shut Them," etc. Visit Web sites that feature children's songs from around the world. Check out www.mamalisa.com.
- Free-dance to music (Dixieland, tango). Interrupt the music once in a while; children must freeze. (Two-year-olds.)
- To help children relax, suggest these stretching exercises. (Two-year-olds.)

  The butterfly: Slowly mime the metamorphosis of a butterfly: caterpillar, cocoon, spreading the wings, first flight. End the activity with something quiet, such as the butterfly resting on a beautiful flower.

  Tickling: Pretend to tickle the ceiling and the walls with arms extended, while keeping the feet and the body vertical. Variation: Combine both actions—tickle the ceiling with one arm and the floor with the other.

  Sun rays: Push away the big black clouds in the sky so that the sun may come out. Then pull the sun rays toward you and place them in your heart or in an imaginary basket. At the end, observe the beautiful blue sky free of clouds.

  Star and planet: Have children lie down, keeping distance between them. Ask them to spread their legs and arms to form a star. Then have them make a ball with their body to form a planet. Alternate a few times between each posture.

The cat: On all fours, stretch like a cat by arching the back up and down. Repeat this movement a few times.

The ladybug: Standing, bent forward, leave relaxed arms hanging and swinging until they come to a complete stop. Imagine a ladybug sitting on your hands and swinging.

The flower: Imitate a flower opening slowly. Start crouching and slowly stretch the arms while getting up on tiptoe.

- Set up a quiet area with cushions, books, and albums to look at alone. Define the quiet area with masking tape on the floor or a tulle curtain hanging from the ceiling. (You may have to tell children not to pull on the curtain.) (Three-year-olds.)

I. BREATHING GAMES (THREE-YEAR-OLDS)

Note: For beginners, three repetitions are enough, while older children can repeat the exercises up to five times. The goal is for children to enjoy the activity, so don't overdo it. Remember that exhaling is the calming phase of breathing because it relieves tension.

- The piglet's nose: Perform an energizing breathing exercise inspired by yoga: Place an index finger lightly on the tip of the nose to make a turned-up nose, breathe through the nose, and then exhale through the mouth while leaving the finger on the nose. Repeat the sequence three to five times. This technique increases awareness of breathing in and out and increases breathing efficiency.

- Candles: Stretch all five fingers of a hand to represent candles. Blow out each candle, and close each finger in turn.

- It smells so good! Pick imaginary flowers and smell each of them before forming a bouquet.

- The sigh: Try to produce exaggerated sighs by raising shoulders (inhaling) and then lowering them (exhaling).

- The wind: Imitate wind sounds by blowing through the mouth: light wind, strong wind, alternate between each.

J. OLFACTORY GAMES (TWO-YEAR-OLDS)

- Make children aware of pleasant smells in the environment. "Something smells nice in the kitchen. What do you think it is?" Smell clean hands after washing them.

- Smell little homemade potpourri bags (hermetically sealed) or little soap bars solidly wrapped in a piece of tulle. Avoid mixing smells; put each material into a resealable plastic bag, then put them all into an attractive box.

K. TACTILE GAMES

- Sitting on the floor, have children draw something with a finger on the back of a partner who will try to guess what it is. Then reverse the roles. Variation: Suggest a theme (shapes, letters, food). This game can be played without the guessing by drawing on someone's back just for the sensory pleasure it provides. (Three-year-olds.)

- Manipulate safe materials with interesting textures. Identify some characteristics—rough, soft, prickly, plastic, fabric, rubber, leather, paper. Variation: Play a guessing game with eyes closed. (Two-year-olds.)

- Have children touch and explore objects placed in a box: elastic, buttons, cotton tips, ribbons, and so forth. Make suggestions such as, "Find something you use when you write." (Four-year-olds.)

L. VOCAL GAMES

- Rap the directions! Children can clap their hands at the same time. (Five-year-olds.)
- Make a megaphone with a cardboard cylinder and speak to the children through it. Hands placed on either side of the mouth can serve the same purpose. (Three-year-olds.)
- Invite children to produce sounds: "I open the window," (open your arms wide) "and I hear . . . a little cat," (birds, wind, etc.). The children imitate the sounds with their mouth, tongue, breath, etc. "I close the window" (close your arms). "The sounds are sleeping." (Two-year-olds.) Variation: Explore various themes: countryside, farm, seaside, city.
- Encourage children to lower their voices and speak as if they have sore throats. Give them an example. (Four-year-olds.)
- Teach children to whisper, and make them aware that vocal chords stay inactive during true whispering. By placing a hand on their throat, children learn that it vibrates when they talk but not when they whisper. (Four-year-olds.)
- Use verbal signals (for example, rally sounds) to help children to be quiet or attentive. (Three-year-olds.)

A call followed by an echo:

Educator's call	Children's response
PARA	CHUTE
CHEWING	GUM
RATADIDADA	DADA
HO HE	HO HE

Suggestions: Pause for five seconds after the children respond before speaking again (in a calm voice). Change the calls regularly to avoid boredom.

- Count backward: 5-4-3-2-1-0-ZIP
- Surprise children by using a toy telephone to simulate receiving a call from a mysterious person. Play the role in a convincing way. "Children, someone on the phone wants to tell us something. . . . I want to hear what he is telling us. . . . Ah, he is telling us it is time to get ready for nap." (Three-year-olds.)
- Invite children to lower their voice by placing a magical finger on their mouth. (Two-year-olds.)
- General laughter. At a signal, pretend to laugh loudly. Then stop at the second signal. Laughter can reduce stress and create complicity within the group. (Five-year-olds.)

> *Avoid the traditional, "Shh, Shh," to request silence or lowering of voices. Used in a repetitive way, this irritates children rather than calming them. It is more effective to provide a good example by lowering your own voice.*

M. ARTISTIC GAMES

- Allow children to scribble on a white board while they are waiting to use the bathroom. (Three-year-olds.)
- Let children draw on a large piece of paper fixed to the wall. Leave the paper out for several days and invite children to draw on it during idle times. Encourage spontaneous drawing without seeking performance or realism. (Three-year-olds.)

Do not use traditional coloring sheets to keep children busy. They stifle children's creativity. It is the same for pre-writing and pre-mathematics exercises. They belong to schoolagers. In early childhood education programs, intellectual force-feeding, early schooling, and hyperschooling have no place. The focus of the curriculum should be on imagination, play, and the development of children's potential.

N. SELF-MASSAGE (TWO-YEAR-OLDS)

- Whipping cream: Wave and shake arms or other parts of the body to make imaginary whipping cream. Then pretend to lather it onto legs, face, hands, and so forth.

- Pizza: Knead the imaginary dough and spread it on legs. Pretend to add tomato sauce and other ingredients (making small circles, tapping, moving fingers, softly touching). Finally, let it bake by lying on the ground.

- A little bit of well-being: Apply a small amount of lotion to the face, hands, and forearms. If a child has skin allergies, use sunscreen provided by the parents. Children particularly like delicate fruity fragrances such as orange or strawberry.

- Delicate sensations: Softly self-massage the cheeks, the neck, the forehead, the ears, and the shoulders.

- Tactile drawing: Have children make an imaginary drawing on their forearm, then erase it. Repeat two or three times.

References

Note: Quotations taken from French-language publications listed below were translated into English by Selma Tischer.

Betsalel-Presser, Raquel, and Denise Garon. 1984. La garderie: Une expérience de vie pour l'enfant. *Volets 1-2-3.* Québec: Les Publications du Québec.

Boisvert, Jovette. 2000. Dis merci! *Le Magazine Enfants Québec* 12 (5):37–40.

Bredekamp, Sue, and Carol Copple. 1997. *Developmentally appropriate practice in early childhood programs. Rev. ed.* Washington, DC: NAEYC.

Brickman, Nancy Altman, and Lynn Spencer Taylor. 1991. *Supporting young learners 1: Ideas for preschool and day care providers.* Ypsilanti, MI: High/Scope Press.

Davidson, Jane. 1982. Wasted time: The ignored dilemma. *Curriculum planning for young children.* Ed. Janet Brown. Washington, DC: NAEYC.

Essa, Eva. 1990. *A practical guide to solving preschool behavior problems.* 2nd ed. Albany: Delmar Publishers.

Hendrick, Joanne. 1988. *The whole child: Developmental education for the early years.* 4th ed. Columbus, OH: Merrill Publishing.

Hohmann, Mary, and David P. Weikart. 1995. *Educating young children: Active learning practices for preschool and child care programs.* Ypsilanti, MI.: High/Scope Press.

Lambert-Lagacé, Louise. 2000. *Feeding your preschooler: Tasty nutrition for kids two to six.* Toronto: Stoddart.

Larose, Andrée. 2000. *La santé des enfants . . . en services de garde éducatifs.* Québec: Les Publications du Québec.

Lauzon, Francine. 1990. *L'éducation psychomotrice: Source d'autonomie et de dynamisme.* Québec: Presses de l'Université du Québec.

Legendre, Renald. 1993. *Dictionnaire actuel de l'éducation.* 2nd ed. Montréal: Guérin.

Martin, Jocelyne, Céline Poulin, and Isabelle Falardeau. 1992. *Le bébé en garderie.* Sainte-Foy, Québec: Presses de l'Université du Québec.

Miller, Darla Ferris. 1990. *Positive child guidance.* Albany: Delmar Publishers.

Papalia, Diane E., Sally Wendkos Olds, and Ruth Duskin Feldman. 1998. *Human development.* 7th ed. Boston: McGraw-Hill.

Petit, Jocelyne. 1997. *Manger avec des enfants: Pour le plaisir et pour la vie.* Sainte-Foy, Québec: Presses de l'Université Laval.

———. 1994. *Manger en garderie: Un art de vivre au quotidien.* Laval, Québec: Éditions Beauchemin.

Pimento, Barbara, and Deborah Kernested. 2004. *Healthy foundations in early childhood settings.* 3rd ed. Toronto: Thomson Nelson.

PROSOM (association nationale de promotion des connaissances sur le sommeil). 2006. http://sommeil.univ-lyon1.fr/PROSOM/index.html.

Thirion, Marie, and Marie-Josèphe Challamel. 1999. *Le sommeil, le rêve et l'enfant: De la noissance à l'adolescence.* 2nd ed. Paris: Albin Michel.

Tyminski, Carroll. 2006. *Your early childhood practicum and student teaching experience: Guidelines for success.* Upper Saddle River, NJ: Pearson/Merrill/Prentice Hall.

Weitzman, Elaine. 1992. *Learning language and loving it: A guide to promoting children's social and language development in early childhood settings.* Toronto: Hanen Centre.

Other Resources from Redleaf Press